Chance of a Lifetime

Nucky Johnson, Skinny D'Amato and How Atlantic City Became the Naughty Queen of Resorts

Grace Anselmo D'Amato
Foreword by Vicki Gold Levi

DOWN
THE
SHORE
PUBLISHING

Harvey Cedars, New Jersey

Down The Shore Publishing Corp.
Box 3100, Harvey Cedars, NJ 08008

www.down-the-shore.com

The words "Down The Shore" and its logos are registered U.S. Trademarks.

Manufactured in the United States of America.
10 9 8 7 6 5 4 3 2 1
First printing, 2001.

Edited by Peggy Ackermann
Book design by Leslee Ganss

Library of Congress Cataloging-in-Publication Data

D'Amato, Grace Anselmo, 1927-
    Chance of a lifetime : Nucky Johnson, Skinny D'Amato and how Atlantic City
    became the Naughty Queen of Resorts / Grace Anselmo D'Amato.
        p. cm.
    Includes bibliographical references (p.   ) and index.
    ISBN 0-945582-75-7
    1. Atlantic City (N.J.)–Politics and government–20th century. 2. Atlantic City
(N.J.)–Social life and customs–20th century. 3. Atlantic City (N.J.)–Economic
conditions–20th century. 4. Johnson, Nucky, 1883-1968. 5. D'Amato, Skinny, d. 1984.
6. Politicians–New Jersey–Atlantic City–Biography. 7. Businessmen–New
Jersey–Atlantic City–Biography. 8. Celebrities–New Jersey–Atlantic City–Biography.
    I. Title.
F144.A8 D36 2001
974.9'85032'0922–dc21
                                    2001042516

*To the memory of my husband,
Emil "Willie" D'Amato, who lived the odyssey
of Atlantic City's heady, exciting and sybaritic days,
and to our three children and five grandchildren,
who have brought us pride in their
accomplishments. I'm grateful to Willie for ignoring
me when I said, "Why don't you get rid
of those photographs?"*

Contents

Foreword

In the 1950s, I grew up in the 500 Club, or at least it felt that way. My Dad, Al Gold, was the official photographer for the celebrity resort, and he augmented his salary by moonlighting at the Five. Dad ran the photography concession, which consisted of snapping the starstruck patrons who composed the wildly enthusiastic 500 Club audiences. Well, he didn't actually do the shooting himself — my Dad had perfumed, glamour gals in high heels and net stockings clicking away for him. Meanwhile, he was holed up in a tiny, chemical-filled darkroom in the back, rapidly developing before the show's finale the souvenir images that proclaimed to all the folks back home that you had actually been to the world-renowned 500 Club. These glossy mementos, nestled in their kitschy photo holders, were proof positive that you really had seen a famous celebrity perform in the flesh — someone like Sophie Tucker, Jimmy Durante, Sammy Davis Jr., the Andrews Sisters, Dean Martin and Jerry Lewis, and maybe, if you were very, very lucky — Frank Sinatra!

Through my Dad's access and club owner Paul "Skinny" D'Amato and his club manager brother Willie's indulgence, I was tolerated hanging around the club and often got quite an eyeful and earful for such a young girl of thirteen. But how I adored the atmosphere. The lush, burgundy velvet curtains that seemed so elegant and decadent at the same time.

The signature zebra motif on the banquettes, napkins and menus that exotically welcomed you into what almost seemed like a private club. And I was fascinated by the regular performers, who lounged around before show time and appeared so sophisticated to me. Young male singers in black tuxedos with their silk bow ties still casually askew, and stunning, leggy chorus girls sporting thick, black, never-ending eyelashes made me eager to grow up and join this exclusive adult world with promises of fame and fortune for its lucky membership.

A photograph of Vicki Gold Levi with Sophie Tucker at the 500 Club in 1953, taken by her father, Atlantic City photographer Al Gold.

While Willie was the sweetest man in the world, and a more behind-the-scenes-get-the-job-done kind of fellow, Skinny was the ultimate cool guy. He had so much charisma that he put most movie stars to shame. His companion cigarette constantly dangled nonchalantly from his lips, and his sleepy, watchful eyes always seemed full of fun and mischief. He was the epitome of swagger, and many a young upcoming male star, including Sinatra, tried to emulate his "I don't ever sweat" style.

I naively felt a certain entitlement at the time to hang out in the hallowed halls of the Five. It just seemed normal to watch Keely Smith and Louis Prima rehearse their hilarious shtick, or the McGuire Sisters run through their melodies. I thought nothing of asking Joey Bishop questions, or Sophie Tucker for her autograph. It seemed perfectly natural to be asked to baby-sit comedian "Fat" Jack E. Leonard's prized Chihuahuas ensconced at the Traymore Hotel on the Boardwalk. When I saw Sammy Davis Jr. frolicking on the beach, I impetuously ran up to him and begged him to imitate Jerry (Lewis) for me and was thrilled, but not surprised, when he did. Why not? The Five was my private stomping grounds, and I proudly brought my friends to see the latest shows and eat a shared steak on those snazzy zebra banquettes. This was Atlantic City in the fifties: fun and gaiety. Everyone came to the Shore to lose their inhibitions and have a good time. And if Frank, and Dean, and Jerry, and Sammy and Zsa Zsa just helped you get in the swinging mood a little bit more — so much the better.

Grace D'Amato has captured all of these happenings and more in her wonderful chronicle of Atlantic City's bawdy past. Reading as a cross between a Damon Runyon short story and a script for a Rat Pack movie, Grace takes you into the center of the action. Breathing life into the political bosses and kingpins of the city's heydays, you can trace the town's rise and fall and rise again like the mythical phoenix from the ashes.

I never realized in my salad days at the 500 Club, the Club Harlem breakfast show and the endless summer days on Steel Pier watching the legendary high-diving horses that I was a witness to a show business era that would never repeat itself. The annals of Atlantic City history welcome this book penned by Grace D'Amato, and her pithy observations about the wink-of-an-eye wickedness that made Atlantic City the undisputed Queen of Resorts — naughty or otherwise.

Vicki Gold Levi
New York, N.Y.

Vicki Gold Levi is the co-author of *Atlantic City: 125 Years of Ocean Madness*, a founder of the Atlantic City Historical Museum on the city's Garden Pier and is a renowned authority on Atlantic City history.

Introduction

In my lifetime, I have watched Atlantic City bewitch the nation as an entertainment capital and first-rate resort, and then be done and left for dead. I have watched this beloved city rise again to reign over the East Coast as a venue for stars to perform and for people of varied economic status to amuse themselves. And I have looked back to a time before my own, to explore the city's history before it repeated itself.

Since the politically active Dr. Jonathan Pitney helped found what was first called Absecon Beach on Absecon Island in the 1830s, Atlantic City's sultry breezes have tempted men. Some were content to splash in her ocean waves. Others sought the cheap thrill of gambling, or the thrill of cheap women. Still others, well beyond feeling any thrill at all, just wanted cheap booze. But the men who were larger than life, men like Enoch L. "Nucky" Johnson, Frank S. "Hap" Farley, and Paul E. "Skinny" D'Amato, these men wanted it all. Like jealous lovers, they needed to possess Atlantic City. In truth, they were possessed by her, the Queen of Resorts.

Nucky, Hap, and Skinny were not ordinary men, and they certainly were not flawless men. They made their own rules, following a code of honor that was loosely based on the Golden Rule and absolutely tolerant of lawlessness on an as-needed basis. All three men were blessed with exaggerated portions of ambition, greed, charisma, and generosity. Legend after legend, these men knew well the Queen's naughty side, and they exploited it every way they could. Sure, they were in it for themselves, but they always gave something back, too. And though they failed to conquer the Queen, they did make her one heck of a "good-time gal" in the process.

Almost anyone will tell you that Atlantic City always has hustled. What had been one of the naughtiest cities is today one of the most regulated, since the approval of legalized gambling in 1976. Skinny D'Amato, incidentally, was instrumental in bringing legalized gambling to the city. He believed it was the key to the city's reinvention, and he was right. Like Nucky and Hap, my rakishly handsome brother-in-law was a lot of things according to a lot of different people. But when it came to Atlantic City, he was a visionary.

Atlantic City today owes its expensive flashiness to Nucky et al., as well as to the men — it's always men with her — who now swoon over her. She drips in wealth on some streets and drowns in poverty on others, an incongruous mixture of sphinxlike hotels with gaudy, noisy casinos, million-dollar condominiums, ramshackle houses, boarded stores, freshly tarred parking lots and buses emitting choking fumes as they carry the hopeful to, and the forlorn from, the gambling halls on which the city has staked its future. The barreling buses vie for limited road space with visitors driving ordinary automobiles and tinted, stretch limousines shrouding big-time gamblers and famous entertainers. After nearly two sad decades of dereliction, from the 1960s into the 1980s, Atlantic City has reclaimed her soul, and she lives again. A different era gives the Queen a new look.

But she is the same underneath, and the same forces are at work, and play, in this city that has had the justifiable audacity to call herself the Queen of Resorts. The sparkling Atlantic Ocean always has been the Queen's biggest lure, followed by an unabashed display of lavishly indulgent excesses of all kinds.

On May 26, 1978, the first legal dice rolled in Atlantic City as Resorts International Hotel Casino opened. Atlantic City now has a dozen casino hotels, many and varied entertainers, a plethora of shows and sights to see, a restored lighthouse on one end, a ballpark on the other and spiffy new housing stock. But she always will be a woman with a past.

For those who recall the bawdy, golden, and elegant era of Atlantic City from the 1920s to the 1960s, please enjoy this nostalgic and flamboyant journey through her storied past. For those who are meeting the Naughty Queen for the first time, beware of her intoxicating powers, and remember that what was considered bad elsewhere was considered good in Atlantic City. And that when it came to badness, the wild, exciting and glamorous Queen had it all: bosses, bootlegging, graft, horse joints, illegal gambling, bordellos and gay bars.

Artist Louis "Boardwalk Louie" Levine, who died in June 1992, had been an Atlantic City resident for seventy years. He gained local notoriety at the 1939 World's Fair as the world's fastest artist, sketching people within two minutes. In his youth, Louie had been a sand artist. He spent his winters in San Miguel de Allende, Mexico, but he came back to Atlantic City every summer. He once was asked, "Why do you return to the island?" His succinct response said it all:

"It's a habit."

And so it is with other islanders, whose shoes are "filled with sand," and who live to breathe the Queen's fresh sea air, nestle their feet in her soft, beige sands, sail their boats and yachts around her island, and lose themselves in the bright lights of her seductive nights.

Now the number of people visiting Atlantic City, some 33 million of them every year, and the growing populations living in her suburbs, have swelled beyond old-timers' imaginations. Longtime city residents stare at the Queen's new jewels with awe. Year-round employment uplifts the spirits of both islanders and newcomers, and the "world's oldest profession" is difficult to stop, despite the efforts of police who now try to do so.

Most people will tell you that the city has come a long way from the dereliction that remained from her last binge of unbridled immorality. Her reputation, they say, has been restored, and even improved. And yet, some islanders say that the old days were better, even with illegal gambling, and tacitly sanctioned prostitution. These islanders will remind you that illicit activities went on behind closed doors, usually between consenting adults, and that families could stroll safe streets anytime.

I remember those days when risk was bought and safety was free, and it is my great pleasure to share these recollections. This book is the result of fourteen years of research and interviews, and of the many more years that I knew my husband, Willie, who was the brother of Skinny D'Amato and the manager of Skinny's 500 Club. Willie brought home some of the most truly incredible, and incredibly true, stories about Atlantic City and her people. This book also contains firsthand accounts of events I thoroughly enjoyed.

Because this book is such a personal account and involves my family, and may even qualify as my fourth child, I have chosen carefully the stories and events that are told. I believe they accurately convey the tale of "old" Atlantic City, the grand and naughty Queen of Resorts. The things that went on there weren't always pretty, but I write about them lovingly because Atlantic City always has had guts and spunk and, most of all, the hearts of those who truly know her.

Now I leave that to you to judge for yourself as you experience the vivaciously salacious days, and nights, that breathed life throughout the Naughty Queen.

Chance of a Lifetime

Part I: Nucky

P eople never have been able to resist Atlantic City. In the late nineteenth century, there were no cars, no highways, and no bridges to bring teeming throngs of humanity to the Absecon Island city. Yet the people came. From the New Jersey mainland, they took skiffs and canoes, and later rode the rails, across bay waters to reach Atlantic City, the resort that was bold enough to lay claim to an entire ocean in its very name.

On the far side of the city, the sound of the waves of the mighty Atlantic Ocean beckoned people like a temptress, promising the indolence of warm beaches and the caress of cooling breezes. People came, and then they came back. Some never left.

Islander Herb Gaskill's people arrived in Atlantic City in the 1850s, when pontoons were used to reach the barrier-island resort. A road eventually was built from Washington Avenue in Pleasantville, on the mainland, across wetlands and the bay to Florida Avenue in Atlantic City. Made of locally abundant pine trees and oyster shells, the island's first thoroughfare was called the "corduroy road" because the half timbers resembled the wales of a corduroy pattern as they lay side by side on the ground. Corduroy also suggested the wordplay of a cord of wood. An unintended translation of corduroy might be "heart of the king."

How appropriate that it should lead to the place that for decades would call itself the Queen of Resorts.

The barrier island's allure, and the accessibility of a road, brought tourists en masse. A boardwalk soon rose, running parallel to the beach and ocean it showcased to allow visitors an admiring seashore stroll. Those who chose not to walk could avail themselves of rolling chairs, conveyances unique to Atlantic City that were pushed by local men looking to earn fast cash and proffered by fiercely dueling companies looking to put each other out of business. Graceful hotels soon lined the Boardwalk, and tourists and islanders personalized an elegant mode of dress. Women wore hats and gloves, while men looked spiffy in Panama hats and carried walking sticks.

During the winter, black tie, evening gowns and furs were *de rigueur*, and islanders and tourists attended New York shows and films at Atlantic City's Warner and Apollo theatres. After the shows, people strolled the Boardwalk, an umbrella of stars glittering above them, and they dined in the many fine restaurants.

Not all was so fine and fancy in Atlantic City, however. Boarding houses accommodated tourists of modest means. Families used communal bathrooms and kitchens, pitching in daily for a block of ice costing ten cents. Bottles of milk were marked off, and accusations of stolen food and milk were pervasive. At times, chaos ruled. Fistfights flared among the forty or so families who shared one kitchen and icebox. If the landlord could not quell the brouhaha, he summoned police.

But to spend one or two weeks on the island, languishing in the sun, swimming in the blue-green waters, was worth the aggravation. The Queen provided visitors gaiety, and solace from their mundane lives. The ocean refreshed their bodies from the sunny city's heat and tempered their minds. Just as it was for the upper classes, Atlantic City was their paradise.

Drivers with horse-drawn carriages that could hold ten people waited at the railroad station for customers. For a dollar a head, they drove them to elegant hotels, where sun-speckled beaches awaited them by day and fine dinners and dancing to orchestra music beckoned by night.

A tlantic City is unique, but it is not alone on Absecon Island. Below it are the cities of Ventnor and Margate, and at the southwestern tip of the island lies the borough of Longport. In the 1920s, a trip across the water to another barrier island, Ocean City, New Jersey, cost twenty-five cents during the summer. Rumrunners, who did quite a business up and down the East Coast, found the Longport-Ocean City route not at all to their liking, however, because the ocean and bay met there in tricky, swirling waters.

Despite the elegance of Atlantic City, and the draw of the ocean, the beach and the Boardwalk, something was missing for tourists who yearned to be as free as the air they breathed. They wanted something more daring, something illicitly delicious, something naughty.

And so the Queen soon tempted her subjects and guests with all the ills they craved: illegal gambling, illegal drinking and illegal women. Upon their arrival on the island, tourists drank, and they played, un-leashing their inhibitions. Islanders tolerated their outrageous behav-ior and catered to their every whim. The Queen increasingly became a place where people could succumb to naughtiness.

In 1908, a corps of policemen and detectives raided a gambling joint. They captured an entire ton of paraphernalia, confiscating rou-lette wheels, faro layouts and spindle games. Gamblers dodged flying bullets and jumped out of second- and third-story windows, landing in piles of rubbish and garbage. According to police, most of the "inmates" escaped. But few arrests were made not because of the gamblers' leap-ing prowess, but rather because some policemen preferred bribes to prisoners.

In 1913, gambling devices valued at tens of thousands of dollars were destroyed at the city dump. Fifty slot machines and poker and African gold tables were smashed and fed to a roaring fire. City officials nodded in satisfaction as the blaze blanketed and lit the Queen's skies with smoke and flames. The following day, the unrepentant — and well-supplied — gamblers were back in action.

The Naughty Queen shunned few people. Among them were ho-bos, some native, some relocated, who had answered the call of the

Queen's lure. Hobos. Gambling. Prostitution. There were those who saw the Queen as an elegant lady being sullied by so much riffraff.

Finally, the *Atlantic City Daily Press* newspaper warned the Queen to "clean up her house," lest outsiders' interfere in her affairs, and the nation begin to consider her incorrigible. The shameless Queen merely laughed at the notion

When Prohibition came along in 1920, it offered Atlantic City yet another way to make money. The Inlet Hotel, located in the northern part of the city, had a pavilion with a yacht landing, from which the Coast Guard patrolled the waters for rumrunners near Absecon Inlet. Despite the Coast Guard's vigilance, the bootleggers were able to outwit them. They dispatched their cohorts in decoy "chase boats" into the ocean, while others delivered liquor to the Atlantic City suburbs of Ventnor, Margate and Longport. Rumrunners' boats had two hundred and fifty horsepower and two outboard motors. As a precaution, they also had mounted machine guns.

On the Black Horse Pike in West Atlantic City stood an elegant Spanish villa. The main entrance was on Lakes Bay, where blazing sunsets shimmered on the water. A romantic scene, yes, but the activities that occurred there were more venal than carnal. Local lore had it that rumrunners used the villa as a base for their illegal activities. They set up a sophisticated telephone system throughout the island to warn their fellow rumrunners of impending raids.

An even better tale had Woolworth heiress Barbara Hutton purchasing the villa for her summer sojourns. After she married movie star Cary Grant on July 8, 1942, locals say, the couple enjoyed moonlit nights there.

The villa changed hands many times. One owner purchased an altar from Mexico for use as a bar. Some people claimed it was a sacrilege, and word spread that the villa was spooked. In time, the villa's only inhabitants became the pigeons, wild cats, bats and rats that peered through its broken windows. The villa still stands today, boarded up, withered and in sore need of demolition.

Back at the inlet, a hubbub of activity went on as rumrunners used garveys and schooners protected by boats on either side. Police watched over the illegal activities run by men such as Enoch "Nucky" Johnson, whose power permeated Absecon Island and Atlantic County during the Roaring Twenties.

N ucky was a handsome, tall, personable young man with a husky voice. As he grew older, his eyes squinted behind tortoise-shell spectacles. A debonair man, he wore custom-made clothes, with a preference for dark blue suits and a fresh, burgundy carnation in his lapel. That trademark carnation distinguished Nucky throughout his life. In cold weather, he kept warm beneath a long raccoon coat.

As Atlantic County's treasurer, Nucky earned six thousand dollars a year, which to him was pin money that he used for gratuities and charity. Islanders speculated he had an unreported income of five hundred thousand dollars a year from illegal gambling, prostitution, payoffs and the flow of whiskey.

According to a 1925 edition of *Who's Who in New Jersey* and to William McMahon, a former newspaperman and the chronicler of area history whose books include *So Young ... So Gay!*, Nucky was born on January 20, 1883, in Galloway Township on the Atlantic County mainland. He was the son of Smith E. and Virginia Higbee Johnson. Nucky was educated in the seat of Atlantic County government, Mays Landing. He graduated from Atlantic City High School in 1900.

In 1904, Nucky became involved in politics, a game he instinctively played well. He became Atlantic County's undersheriff when he was only twenty-one years old, and in 1908, at age twenty-five, he was elected county sheriff. Nucky served as sheriff for one term. He was elected Atlantic County treasurer in 1914, and from that time until his downfall almost thirty years later in 1941, he possessed impregnable power.

He had moxie, too. In 1915, state Senator Walter Evans Edge, a Republican and founder of the *Atlantic City Press* morning newspaper, asked Nucky to head his gubernatorial campaign. Edge handed Nucky ten thousand dollars. Two months later, Nucky asked Edge — who in 1916 would win the governor's job with the biggest plurality ever for a New Jersey gubernatorial candidate — for an additional ten thousand dollars.

"Nucky, you're my campaign manager, not an international financier," Edge protested.

Nucky roared with laughter. He and Edge dined and discussed campaign strategies. Pushing himself away from the table, Nucky excused himself.

"I have a rendezvous with a fair-haired lady called Morpheus," he said.

"Morpheus? Nucky, that's a man's name", Edge replied, recalling the god of dreams from Greek mythology.

"Yes, but she's a fair-haired beauty," Nucky assured.

Edge nodded. Nucky's obsession with women was both insatiable and legendary.

Nucky was a very public and gregarious person. He was everywhere and had his hand in everything. He was a playboy one moment and a practical and disciplined political boss the next. And yet, there was an enigmatic quality to him. He was a devotee of religion who studied mysticism in various denominations. Protestant by birth, he found great comfort in the Catholic Mass. Nucky wasn't picky about his spiritual associations, or his corporeal ones, either.

In 1929, Nucky entertained gangsters at a convention in Atlantic City. They were famous or infamous men, according to the side one had chosen, and included Frank Costello; Meyer Lansky; Charles "Lucky" Luciano; Arthur Flegenheimer, who was better known as Dutch Schultz; and Alphonse "Scarface" Capone.

Nucky lived in the fashionable Ritz-Carlton Hotel, which he eventually purchased, on Iowa Avenue on the Boardwalk. He accommodated his guests across the street at the President Hotel with the prettiest, sexiest girls and the best whiskey. Because he owned houses of prostitution, and profited from others who ran their free-style bordellos, numbers rackets, and horse parlors, he could afford to be a gracious and genial host.

Nucky greatly enjoyed walks along the Boardwalk, and he frequently strolled the wood-planked way with his guests. He dressed in fine-tailored suits, and islanders rendered him and his entourage homage, awed by their money and power. Those men spent freely, and tipped generously, and islanders catered to their needs.

Although the notorious presence of the gangsters caused some trepidation among local residents, curiosity seekers could not be kept from the resort. Atlantic City was "wide open" and rather accepting of vice. It offered both top-quality entertainment and carnival-type acts — such as Siamese-twin sisters and midget boxing — and it had the seashore. Business flourished, and coins jingled in the Naughty Queen's pockets.

In the early twenties, Nucky owned the Silver Slipper Supper Club, a classy joint, where men actually drank champagne out of beautiful showgirls' silver high heels. Two of the main attractions were Gilda Gray, the "Shimmy Queen," and Evelyn Nesbit, a showgirl who married the neurotic, jealous millionaire, Henry "Harry" Kendall Thaw.

A famous architect named Stanford White fell in love with Evelyn and threatened her marriage. Thaw ended that threat by shooting and killing White in 1906 at Madison Square Garden in New York. Out of his passion for Evelyn, White had built her a swing in his home and padded it with red velvet. Thus Evelyn Nesbit gained notoriety as "the girl in the red velvet swing," whose husband had shot her lover out of implacable rage.

Islanders and tourists relished dancing in nightclubs, gambling illegally, boozing and womanizing. In many ways, they acted like unsupervised teenagers. And those who really were teenagers acted on their impulses as well.

In one common activity, local boys and girls would hop into a friend's car and cruise through "Prostitutes Alley" on South Chalfonte Avenue. The girls crouched on the floor in back of the car, giggling, and occasionally peeking to see what was happening. The boys gawked at the working girls who displayed their sensual bodies as they waved and beckoned the young men to spend some time, and money, on South Chalfonte.

Now the boys were in heat, and they knew the going rate was fifty cents, or a dollar if the girl was young and exceptionally pretty. They emptied their pockets and came up with a dollar. Next came a nickel toss, and the winner had the distinction of being the first to enter the so-called "well of Venus."

One man recalling his youth said winning the nickel toss was the first defining experience of his manhood. He opened the door to a bordello, and a pretty, shapely blonde swung her hips, luring him into her arms. But the madam pushed her away and stood before him. Her brassy red hair was piled on top of her head, her wrinkled face was painted with rouge and her lipstick lapped over her lips. Her etched bosom popped out of her green dress. She puffed a cigarette. Her palm was open and extended.

"Buster, anything special?" she asked.

"Ugh ... ugh ..." he responded.

"Ain't you done it before?" she grinned.

He blushed, shook his head and lowered his eyes. He was a football player, unafraid of anyone on the field. But now his knees wobbled.

"No Ma'am," he said.

She burst out laughing, chuckling still as she signaled the blonde who had accosted him when he entered the house.

"One dollar," the madam said. "Have fun."

"Honey, what's your name?" the blonde inquired when they were alone in a room.

"I'd rather not say," he replied.

She shrugged, put on the radio, swigged some whiskey, and lit a cigarette. She disrobed, and stood naked before him. He looked away.

"Ain't you ever seen a naked lady before? Say, how old are you?"

"Seventeen."

"I'm eighteen," she said.

She led him to the bed, watched him as he undressed and eyed him up and down. His muscles rippled, and she touched his chest.

"Let's get it over with," she said.

"Isn't there hugging and kissing first?"

"Are you kidding? No kissing. What do you want for a dollar?"

Suddenly he felt nauseous, and he glanced at the door. He wanted to run out, but he couldn't waste a whole dollar. And what would he tell his friends? He stared at the ceiling while she worked on him. When it was over, he ran to the bathroom and vomited. Her harsh laughter reverberated throughout the room, unnerving him. He couldn't tell his friends that the only emotion he had was revulsion. He had to make something up, or his friends would think him unmanly.

He glanced at the girl with disdain.

"Why do you do this?" he asked.

"I have to eat … say, are you some kind of do-gooder?"

He shook his head and bolted, running outside and down the steps. The expectant faces of his friends awaited him, and lie after lie poured forth from his mouth. The boys' faces glowed with excitement as they chose the next candidate for the following week.

Nucky Johnson maintained orderly houses of prostitution. He hired a man called "Dr. Ducky," who examined the girls weekly for diseases and performed abortions. The doctor was a nervous man. He smoked ten packs of unfiltered cigarettes a day, lighting one from another. His clump of gray hair had turned orange from the nicotine.

At Nucky's residence on the seventh floor of the Ritz-Carlton Hotel, one closet was full of cash. Those who needed money were welcome to it, but Nucky's men counted it carefully and marked down the amount, with the interest due. In fact, Nucky often peeled off money for those who were destitute and needed cash for their children's shoes, clothing, medication, or an operation. Secure in his power, Nucky only wanted adulation, and lots of it, in return for those acts of charity.

He was pleased by the things people said about their patron:

"Nucky's great!" "Nucky's good-hearted." "Nucky's cordial, polite, a real gentleman." "Atlantic City would be nothing without him."

In fact, his various illegal activities did not disparage his reputation one bit. A benevolent emperor could not have been more beloved than he was.

Few even criticized Nucky's nepotism. When his father and brother took turns as sheriff of Atlantic County, laws were changed to fit the occasion. Politicians bowed to Nucky as well because he kept their coffers filled with money collected from horse joints and brothels. Two hundred dollars per week from each joint was "protection money."

And Prohibition was anything but in Atlantic City. Whenever a cache of burgundy arrived on the smugglers' boats, the rumrunners who worked for Nucky catered to his particular love for the stuff. In addition to his rumrunners, Nucky also hired a man called "Doc Coward." Doc was a pharmacist who forced other pharmacists to order an extra five gallons of whiskey every week so that bootleggers could cut it and make three bottles out of two. They then sold that whiskey as "cheap booze." Naturally, pharmacists complied with Doc Coward's request because a visit from Nucky's men could be dangerous.

According to numerous reports, and local lore, Nucky sent turkeys and food baskets to poor islanders, regardless of color or creed, for Thanksgiving and Christmas. In addition, he purchased coal, and clothing, and contributed to every church and religious institution. His money benefited all the subjects of the Naughty Queen's domain.

Rumors spread throughout New Jersey that Nucky and Mayor Frank "I Am The Law" Hague of Jersey City controlled the state. The gossip also held that Nucky had a vendetta against Hague, although Nucky was not known locally to be a vindictive man. If it were true, perhaps it was no more than that each man wanted total control of the state.

There were wide differences in each man's personality, as well as in their views of what New Jerseyans wanted — and needed. Nucky wanted Atlantic City to be a haven for pleasure-seekers. He himself enjoyed drinking alcoholic beverages and spending evenings in nightclubs with beautiful women. Not so for Hague, who prided himself on his fervent morality, abstained from liquor and tobacco and was sometimes considered a "sourpuss." Neither Hague nor Nucky tried to be kind to each other. It was said that Hague had observed derisively that "Johnson lives like a prince on his salary of six thousand dollars a year."

Regardless of what was or was not said, the men did have a certain regard, if not respect, for each other's power. For his part, Nucky remained a revered, beloved figure in Atlantic City. It appeared that he feared no one — but perhaps he just kept his fears to himself.

Author Harry Duke, who self-published *Neutral Territory*, an unauthorized book about the old Atlantic City rackets, said he was a friend of Nucky rival Nick Scarduccio, otherwise known as Nick Sky.

Sky, one of eight children, fought Nucky's dominant rule over the city to get his own piece of the action. He was rather good-looking in a rugged way with dark hair and dark eyes. It was alleged that Sky was a dangerous man, but he had one soft spot by Atlantic City standards. The story went that Sky refused to sell "rot-gut" booze because his brother Johnny drank bad alcohol that Nucky's bootleggers sold him and died from poisoning. The loss of his brother apparently made Sky a determined man — and Nucky's enemy.

Shortly thereafter, Nick Sky became a successful businessman who dealt in high-grade whiskey. He transported it on huge vessels and used equipment that allowed his men to unload the cargo within ten minutes. This was a clever method for those days, employed more for convenience than stealth: Buyers waited openly on the docks while Sky's men tasted the liquor and counted cases as off-duty policemen stood guard to prevent thefts of the contraband.

Nucky warned his men to keep their distance from Sky, but one disagreed with "the Boss." He was Nucky's top gun, Samuel "Cappy" Hoffman.

Hoffman feared no one, and his appearance alone was enough to terrify anyone. His entrance into joints caused many a dealer's knees to wobble in fear and afforded him the utmost respect. He had a deep, ugly bullet-hole scar on his forehead, which he did not get from being a nice guy.

Meanwhile, Sky apparently was not satisfied with merely his liquor business. He was a thief who specialized in safes. One evening, he entered a house and found a note had been left for him near the safe.

"Please don't ruin my safe, there's no money in it," the note pleaded.

Nick obliged and spared his would-be victim.

Duke claimed that Sky and his brother Jesse were framed and then arrested on trumped-up charges. Because Nucky Johnson controlled the police department, it was a logical conclusion that he was behind the arrests, and that gnawed at Nick and Jesse Scarduccio. Sky worried Nucky, and when he and his brother went to prison, Nucky slept a lot better. But Sky wasn't going to be in prison forever.

One late afternoon, as dusk pulled the color from the sky, Nucky strolled the Boardwalk with dignitaries in evening clothes and top hats. Suddenly Nucky spotted Nick Sky coming toward him. He panicked and turned tail, running away like an ordinary coward. His top hat flew off, and the dignitaries stared at him, bewildered and astonished at his behavior. It was rather unbelievable: Nucky, who had power, wealth and friends beyond his wildest dreams, was displaying fear and running from another man.

From then on, Nucky had hallucinations about Sky and Jesse. Police constantly invaded the Scarduccios' home, looking for Sky, who usually was asleep.

A tragedy arose from the feud between Nucky and Sky when yet another brother, Victor, was shot between his eyes by a bullet meant for Sky. Whoever killed Victor Scarduccio had shot the good son in the family. With the murder of his brother, Sky's fury soared, and his hatred of Nucky shrouded him day and night.

Nucky redoubled his vigilance. He instructed his men and the police to stand guard on the seventh floor of his hotel. He ordered the police to check everyone out before allowing them admittance to the elevator. Nucky did not like violence, preferring to deal from the standpoint of power, amiability and diplomacy. His henchman acted differently, however, and considered drastic steps were needed, at times, to maintain order.

A few weeks later, Jesse Scarduccio shot a detective and was sent back to prison. Sky was arrested on extortion charges and joined his brother in prison. Nucky's nightmares finally ended. Sky died in jail, purportedly under mysterious circumstances. Jesse eventually came home and spent his days quietly, with the utmost respect accorded him.

B usiness in the early 1920s continued as usual in the Naughty Queen's domain. Bookies paid two dollars a week for wire services to obtain race results. Customers had one in one thousand chances of having winning numbers. If they won, they were paid seven hundred dollars for each dollar, which islanders considered fair odds.

Every barber shop, grocery store, candy store and ice cream parlor had bookies. Unemployed islanders who walked the city streets or slept underneath the Boardwalk had a choice: Book numbers or starve.

An influential man and another of the island's unique mosaic of characters was Dan Bastian. He owned a speakeasy called the Lotus Club, which was located on Illinois Avenue above Atlantic Avenue. Politicians and racketeers called him "the judge." He was a large, husky, distinguished, dapper man with wavy gray hair. Prostitutes and gay people called him "Mother Bastian" because he looked after them when they got into trouble and needed money. But he also was a tough man who took no nonsense from anyone.

Although his place was a hangout for the Mafia, he maintained his independence and did not ask for favors. When queried, his comment about the Mafia was the practical response of a businessman: "Friends in the Mafia are like having the protection of the United States Army."

According to author Duke, Dan Bastian's clientele included the dregs of the criminal world. They were con men, thieves, pickpockets, pimps, loan sharks, prostitutes and madams. The more respectable patrons included entertainers who would perform for pay at the Steel Pier and the Garden Pier, and then end the night at Bastian's place, playing to the house gratis.

The only employees Bastian paid were his bartenders and dealers; the rest worked solely for tips. Another thing for which he did not pay was electricity. That he got by tying his wires to the Somers Lumber Company next door. Later on, after he had closed his club, he managed the renowned Club Harlem on North Kentucky Avenue.

Speakeasies like Bastian's depended on the skill and daring of rumrunners. In the late 1920s, according to one-time resident Richard "Smitty" Smith, bootleggers used local waterways, taking care to avoid the hawk-eyed United States Coast Guard. The waters of Brigantine, a barrier island to the north of Atlantic City, were considered safer than some others. But there were no guarantees, and rumrunners needed plans, and backup plans, and the nerve to risk their own lives for the sake of their cargo.

One evening, as the moon glistened over the water, bootleggers detected the sound of a ship over the noises of their own boats. It was the Coast Guard! The rumrunners turned their boat motors off. They quietly unwound ropes, girded their waists and pulled their boats out to sea to wait while the Coast Guard moored its ship.

At times, those motivated men swam beyond Atlantic City's famous sites, Garden Pier, Steel Pier and Million Dollar Pier, eventually reaching Ventnor and Margate, where they unloaded their cargo. The men were exhausted, but they were pleased, too, that their cargo was intact. Their swimming skills and stamina were admirable, considering it was a very long swim of about eight miles.

Evangelists complained about the abominable conditions in the city. According to the *Atlantic City Daily Press*, they paraded the Boardwalk, protesting to the authorities they met that: "Atlantic City must cease the poisonous, foul and putrid streams of persons entering the city with their gambling and drinking."

The authorities listened and nodded politely, pacified them and departed to attend to issues they considered more relevant — often the very things about which the evangelists were complaining.

The evangelists persisted, however, evoking biblical comparisons and further declaring, "There were a few good men in Sodom, and there are a few good men in Atlantic City."

The evangelists did not realize that those few good men in Atlantic City needed forbidden fruit — gambling, drinking and prostitution — along with the tourists who sought respite from their ordinary lives.

There was no doubt that Nucky Johnson considered himself what everyone called him, "Boss," and that nothing went on in the city without his knowledge and permission. Making betting on numbers accessible, day and night, was a priority for him.

Winning numbers were determined by the payouts for different races at various tracks. For example, say the digit to the left of the decimal was the predetermined important number:

$68.00 was paid in the first race at racetrack A.

$29.20 was paid in the second race at track B.

$19.60 was paid in the third race at track C.

The winning number, then, would have been eight hundred ninety-nine.

Atlantic City was known as the "World's Famous Playground" and the "Queen of Resorts." Naturally, famous people flocked to the resort, and the famous columnist Walter Winchell often visited. He wrote in his "On Broadway" column: "If the most beautiful woman in a place is with a man, that man is Enoch 'Nucky' Johnson."

Nucky was delighted. He lived to squire beautiful women, as well as to amass power, and powerful friends such as reporters, congressmen, senators and governors.

The local Morals Betterment League was not so taken with Nucky's employment opportunities for women, however. One day, two members called upon Nucky at his county treasurer's office. They demanded that he close down Minnie Wickle's house of ill repute. Minnie's bordello was considered the most exclusive house on the island, a fact that did not impress the morals league.

Nucky's pleasant smile turned to a grin.

"Who is she?" he inquired innocently. "I'm totally ignorant."

The members of the league bore the brunt of the awkward moment.

"Why she's a procuress ... a madam," one stammered. "She runs a house of ill repute. It's rumored ... we heard you're ..."

"Aw hell, you're wasting your time," Nucky said. "You're intelligent enough to know I can't go around accusing Madam Wickle, or Wiggle, whatever her name is, on rumors and hearsay. They used to burn witches in Salem, but we can't have that in our fair city. Now, gentlemen, go and get me firsthand information. Good day!"

The minute they departed, Nucky notified Minnie.

"There's a guy with a wart on the side of his nose, and another with bushy red eyebrows. They're coming over. Fix them up, then call the police to raid the place while they're still there. I'll pay for the damages."

"Okay, Nuck."

That had the desired effect of stopping the do-gooders for a while. All these years later, old-timers still chuckle when they recall Nucky's naughty little prank.

No one doubted Nucky's astute, intelligent and analytical mind. During World War I, he sold Liberty Bonds to audiences he had charmed. At one of those rallies, Governor Edge, who possessed the long memory of a politician, proposed a toast to Nucky.

"To Enoch 'Nucky' Johnson," Edge said, "great leader and politician, but too expensive."

The audience roared. Appointed by Edge, Nucky served one term as clerk of the New Jersey Supreme Court. But he never sought an elected office outside of Atlantic County. He didn't have to; from his seaside stronghold in Atlantic City he was one of the most powerful men in the state, and his lucrative activities in the Naughty Queen needed his undivided attention.

Nucky was drafted during World War I, but the war ended before he was able to join it. The boss smiled and stayed home to tend his turf. He was approached one day at work by a man who appeared troubled and uneasy.

"Ike, what's wrong?" Nucky asked him.

"Nucky, we've got a dragon for you to slay."

"What happened?"

"Charlie DePaur was eligible for an appointment, but because he's colored, they're passing him up."

Nucky glanced at Isaac Nutter, aggrieved at what he heard. Then his gravelly voice boomed throughout the hallway, so much so that employees ran out of their offices to see what was happening.

"I don't care if he's black or pink!" Nucky bellowed. "See that he's appointed right away! Things like that get under my skin!"

The following week, DePaur reported for work as a clerk in the Atlantic County offices, and thus Nucky institutionalized a patronage system that acknowledged black Republican Party faithful as it had their white counterparts. Still, the new rewards program didn't go over well with everyone. A delegation of white employees marched into Nucky's office.

"Mr. Johnson, there are sixty of us who can help you over the hurdles, but we've never worked with a Negro."

"Times are changing," Nucky answered dismissively.

"But Mr. Johnson, we do not intend to work with that man. Mr. DePaur goes, or we do, right now."

"Suit yourselves. I'll call the Civil Service Commission and ask them to send sixty new hands. That's all, ladies and gentlemen."

The employees swallowed their pride and prejudice. After a few weeks, they invited DePaur to lunch with them.

Nucky's foresight in developing inclusionary policies may have had altruistic elements. It most certainly had a practical basis. Atlantic City had a population of some 66,000 during Nucky's tenure, about half the county's population, which allowed the Boss to control both city and county, according to "The Case of Enoch L. Johnson," a 1943 report by the federal Treasury and Justice departments of the investigation that eventually led to Nucky's downfall.

Of the city's people, approximately 30,000 were black. Nucky recognized that the black vote was essential to balance his power base. He solicited that vote energetically, and he controlled it completely. He also left nothing to chance:

"... When necessity required it, Johnson could always count on a large number of gamblers, prostitutes and floaters to cast sufficient illegal votes for his candidates to supplement the Negro vote," the government's report said. "In addition, Johnson, through his patronage powers, gained control of a sizeable block of votes made up of all county and city employees, their families and friends."

Nucky's inclusion of the city's black residents in patronage positions would be continued by his successor, and would help him build a nearly invincible political machine as well.

With the advent of Prohibition in 1920, many nightclubs had closed their doors, but Nucky and his associates opened new clubs with first-class gambling houses and top-notch entertainment. The list of performers included Jimmy Durante, Ukelele Ike, Joe Venuti, Nick Lucas, and Hilda Ferguson, who was enamored of Nucky, his charm and his money. George Raft was another name in town, and he was enamored of Hilda — losing his ardor only when he discovered that Nucky dated her. Though he was called the "Latin Lover," Raft's original name was Raftt, and he was not of Italian, but rather German, descent.

There were more big names, too: Sophie Tucker, the Red Hot Mama, performed, as did Helen Morgan, who sang while seated at a piano and fluttered her handkerchief against her face. Other players included Peaches Browning and, of course, "Shimmy Queen" Gilda Gray and Evelyn Nesbit of red-velvet-seat fame. Performer Texas Guinan was famous for a "Hello, sucker" salutation to customers that would drench the club in her husky voice.

So much talent, and so much potential for larger audiences to enjoy it — and spend money in the city — gave rise to thoughts of how to capitalize on the opportunity. One version of history credits Nucky with the idea of a convention hall. By another account, the proposition had been around for about a decade when Atlantic City Mayor Edward L. Bader backed a public referendum on the hall in the November 1923 general election. A majority of voters supported the referen-

Long dresses and black stockings were once common beach attire.

Visitors meander along the Boardwalk near Adams's Bathhouse in the 1880s.

Horse-drawn buggies and people move along Virginia Avenue in the 1900s.

Trolley lines, cars and bicycles are all part of the traffic of Atlantic Avenue in 1927.

King Neptune, with the Golden Mermaid Trophy at his feet, crowns Miss America 1926, Norma Smallwood.

Mary Campbell, Miss America 1922 and 1923, was allowed to succeed herself before the pageant rules were changed.

35

Haddon Hall horse stand in spring 1932.

Stars of the 1920s: Happy Thompson, the Blind Tenor, and Rudolph Valentino, accepting the key to the city.

Edward L. Bader, Atlantic City's mayor from 1920-1927. Right, sand artists create a sculpture of a car and passengers, about 1917.

View of Atlantic City hotels on the shoreline.

Atlantic City High School in 1930; it was demolished in May 1999.

Shirley Temple in "Captain January" headlines at Steel Pier in the 1930s.

Aerial view of four piers in 1960, from bottom: Steel, Steeplechase, Central and Million Dollar.

The Six Hustreis perform a tightrope act at Steel Pier in 1931.

39

The Traymore Hotel commands the shoreline here in

the late 1930s. The hotel would be blasted down in 1972.

The crowd notices the camera while waiting on Steel Pier in 1930.

John Philip Sousa (center) with his band and fans at Steel Pier in 1931.

There's something for everyone: dancing, circus acts, vaudeville and more in 1930.

Boxing cats were a popular animal act of the 1930s.

A performer emerges from the sea on one of the famed diving horses in the 1940s.

Prizefighter Primo Carnero boxes with a kangaroo in the 1930s.

A "Little People" show is held in Atlantic City in the 1930s.

Convention Hall in a football-field configuration in 1940.

The Steel Pier Ballroom, top, features the Eddie Nelson Orchestra. Rolling chairs stream along the Boardwalk in the early 1940s.

Well-dressed gentlemen and ladies on the Boardwalk near the Stanley Theatre in the 1930s. Below, separate images of tourist speedboats and the ocean skyline are merged in an eye-catching promotional photograph of the 1930s.

Paul E. "Skinny" D'Amato, left, and a friend outside Skinny's first "joint" in 1922.

dum, and architects Lockwood, Greene and Co. submitted the first plans for the hall a year later. The plans were redrafted continually until July 1926. Demolition contracts to clear the land were awarded, as were contracts to bolster the beachfront location so that it would be able to support the unprecedented structure.

When Atlantic City Convention Hall was dedicated on May 31, 1929, just a few months before the nation's economy collapsed into the Great Depression, it rose like the Roman Coliseum above the Boardwalk and ocean between Mississippi and Georgia avenues. Lest anyone miss the new hall, stone spindles the color of sand overlooked the ocean on the beach side of the Boardwalk. The Boardwalk in front of the building was extended into a semicircle to accommodate the decorative spindle structure and create a grand entrance to a place of grandeur. At fifteen million dollars, Convention Hall had cost a fortune to build.

The hall was big enough for criticism, and big enough to take it. So was Nucky. Ridicule of the extravagant project, and of Nucky for his grandiose ideas, was rampant. But time has proved those who doubted wrong as countless conventions and shows have brought visitors and their dollars to the city, and a second, bigger convention center was built in the 1990s. The most famous, and enduring, show of all, the Miss America Pageant, was held for the first time in Atlantic City Convention Hall in September 1940. The annual pageant has been held there continually since the end of World War II. During the war, the armed forces had used the hall for training purposes.

Nucky also envisioned highways leading into the city. Those who take the Black Horse Pike (U.S. Route 40) or the White Horse Pike (U.S. Route 30) into town can thank Nucky for his foresight, which benefited both the city and the county.

Atlantic County was a place Nucky knew well, both top-side and underside. Growing up as the son of the county sheriff, Nucky was raised on the mainland in Mays Landing, the county seat that was home to both the courthouse and the jail. Nucky often kidded about his formative years "in jail." His ethnic background was Scots-Irish, and he inherited his mother's temperament for charity and education.

Nucky's mother, Virginia, had her own flamboyant personality. She wore high boots decorated with metal toeplates as she drove her produce wagon to the farmer's market in Atlantic City. At times, she enjoyed watching the rumrunners, who used oyster and clam garveys and schooners, unloading her son's whiskey while police stood guard.

In the evening, when she and her husband dined out, Virginia was bedecked in elegant evening gowns, furs and high heels. She was known to indulge in an occasional highball. It was apparent that Nucky got his love of politics from his mother, who relished such discussions, and arguments.

When Virginia Johnson died at eighty-one years of age, funeral services were held at the courthouse in Mays Landing, with several thousand people in attendance. Nucky had covered his mother's casket with a blanket of white orchids. Fifteen cars filled with flowers followed the cortege to the cemetery.

Unlike his father, Nucky loved the theater. He recalled that his father never attended a Broadway show, explaining: "Abraham Lincoln went to the theater and got himself shot. Let that be a lesson to you." As he was unaware of a president who drank himself to death, Nucky's father was comfortable with binges of alcohol. And when he went on his drinking sprees, his boots never came off. They had cost him one hundred dollars, and woe to anyone who tried to remove them.

As a young man, Nucky fell in love with and married, on Sept. 12, 1907, a tall, willowy girl of quiet beauty and intelligence named Mabel Jeffries. She soon became ill with tuberculosis, and her doctor advised Nucky to take her to Denver, Colorado. Perhaps the air coming off the Rocky Mountains would be beneficial to her and save her life.

Nucky found Colorado unbearable, but he placed Mabel's needs above his own. She died in Denver in 1913, and Nucky never felt so alone. He returned to Mays Landing with her body and memories of their love. Nucky sought solace in the arms of other women. Many a damsel remembered glorious nights near the Great Egg Harbor River, when the moon glowed and the stars shone for Nucky and his current paramour.

Years later, a lady whose name has been lost to time wrote: "Ah, if I could only see those magic lights again, flickering on the Great Egg Harbor River, take a carriage ride up Sugar Hill and down Gravelly Run in Mays Landing to the old sawmill for a tryst. I'd love to walk once again beneath venerable oaks, beside the handsome Enoch Johnson, whose sparkling black eyes made many a maiden's heart skip a beat."

Nucky had many public roles, and salaries. He had been sheriff of Atlantic County, but he found the work too confining; he had been clerk of the New Jersey Supreme Court, but he loved Atlantic City, the Boardwalk, the beach and the ocean. Atlantic City was where the action was.

He was a man of the evening who needed a woman's vitality, her softness and her tenderness. His dark eyes twinkled behind tortoise-shell glasses. His husky voice reverberated throughout cabarets, and his presence gave a certain importance to those nightclubs he frequented.

Nucky retired at five or six o'clock in the morning, and his valet, bodyguard and confidante, Louie Kessel, awoke him at four o'clock in the afternoon. Louie pounded Nucky's six-foot frame and rubbed him with ointments and wintergreen oil. Then Nucky showered and had a pot of coffee, along with the usual breakfast his cook prepared for him: a dozen eggs, ham or bacon and homemade biscuits. His closet contained one hundred suits, and he wore spats over black patent leather shoes. Of course, his finishing touch was his burgundy boutonniere.

Louie Kessel, also known as Roly-Poly Louie, was of Russian descent and weighed two hundred and sixty pounds. He often sang and danced to the music of the Cossacks. He had been a wrestler before Nucky hired him, and he also was known as the "Mad Russian."

Nucky purchased a villa across the street from his Ritz-Carlton Hotel. The home was a two-story affair on Iowa Avenue, near the beach. He often strolled the Boardwalk with islanders constantly greeting him. Women smiled, and men doffed their hats.

Soon after he had moved into his villa, a woman friend drove up to the house in a Rolls-Royce. She presented him with the automobile as a gift. Nucky was moved by her generosity and thanked her. She was said to have commented that "He's the first man I'd rather give to than receive from."

Louie, who would be the car's driver, had an idea.

"Boss, how about if we paint it red, and paint 'The Boss' in gold letters?"

"That's some idea," Nucky replied. "No."

Nucky's activities were not limited to Atlantic City. He often traveled to New York City, and a *New York Post* columnist wrote,

"Nucky is one of the most liberal and carefree spenders of the day. He's happy when he has an army of friends and acquaintances around him."

Despite his high-style living, with two Cadillacs, a Lincoln, his Rolls-Royce and a limousine, Nucky supported many charitable endeavors in his beloved Atlantic City. He set up funds for the needy, and blacks loved him because he showed them affection and respect.

In return, islanders did not resent Nucky's luxurious lifestyle. Many believed he needed to maintain a certain standard of living to impress resort visitors properly.

But Nucky's benevolence did have its limits. He found himself forced to dismiss Samuel "Cappy" Hoffman after Cappy was arrested on charges concerning narcotics, concealing a deadly weapon and white slavery. Nucky hated narcotics and junkies, and he told Cappy, who was a drug user: "As long as you confine your killing to your own kind, it's fine with me. In your kind of business, it's dog eat dog."

"I'm the top dog," Cappy replied hotly.

"Maybe in your kennel," Nucky retorted.

Cappy did have a reputation. The *New York Journal* reported:

Cappy Hoffman has a predatory nature, schooled in the classroom of violence. He's been through scenes and passages that even Dante could not describe. His alma mater was a nightmare of horrors.

Cappy was known as the "hatchet man." He was of slight stature and had a sallow, pimpled complexion. Behind his spectacles, there was a fixed, malevolent gaze that terrified his enemies. In earlier years, he had met a bullet upon leaving a building in Philadelphia. The deep gouge the bullet left above his left eye crisscrossed another scar on his forehead.

With Cappy gone, Nucky went on as before. Never a man to miss an opportunity, he backed Broadway-bound shows at the Apollo Theatre and other Atlantic City venues. As the biggest tryout town on the East Coast, shows such as *George White's Scandals*, *Follies Bergere*, in which Evelyn Nesbit performed; *Ziegfeld Follies*, and *Earl Carroll's Vanities* played in Atlantic City before going to Broadway and gaining widespread acclaim.

Once again, evangelists paraded the Boardwalk, complaining about the notorious Chalfonte Alley that encompassed the area near Chalfonte-Haddon Hall. On the north side of Chalfonte Alley, men had their choice of black women; on the south side, white women accommodated them.

Notorious bars and nightclubs included the Gay Pansy Club and the Purple Club. The Entertainers Club on Snake Alley was a cheater's paradise. Snake Alley's name came less from the sort of people who frequented it than from the way it wound through South New York Avenue below Kentucky and Pacific avenues and was somewhat hidden.

The owner of the Entertainers Club was Louise Mack, a former *Ziegfeld Follies* girl who had a habit of sweeping the bar clean whenever her customers went to the bathroom. If they were sober, they would question her upon their return about the absence of their money. She would glance down, grin and tell them, "Honey, your money fell into the ice bucket."

In truth, she would slide the money into the ice bucket and retrieve it after closing. Soggy dollars were later hung on the clothesline in her apartment to dry.

Club Madrid, on Georgia and Arctic avenues, had Atlantic City's first transvestite show in the thirties; the Jockey Club on S. North Carolina Avenue had a gay show with straight customers. Billie Holiday and Ethel Waters performed at the Wonder Gardens on Illinois and Baltic avenues, and the Paradise Club, owned by the Abrams family, had a black show with a mixture of races in attendance.

During the summer, rolling-chair operators pushed their fares to the Paradise Club for the breakfast show, despite the fact that rolling chairs were prohibited on the streets. The Naughty Queen's subjects were known to flout the rules, indulge themselves and change laws to suit the occasion — all with Nucky's approval.

Young men laboring on the highways on the mainland town of Absecon sometimes were overcome with sexual urges. No problem: they made their way to Atlantic City at lunchtime, had a rendezvous with a prostitute and then resumed work.

The girls who made their living in the city's cathouses tended to be runaways or ostracized by their families. Lacking skills and education, they became prostitutes. Joseph D'Amico, a tailor and cleaner whose business was located at Illinois and Atlantic avenues, felt compassion for the girls. He cleaned and altered their clothes at no charge. He gave them money and urged them to return home or find some kind of legitimate work. For all too many of the girls, leaving prostitution simply was an impossibility.

Throngs of girls were lured to the so-called glamour of the Naughty Queen's domain with hopes of being discovered for a Broadway show or, even better, by a rich man. But all too often, their auditions became lessons from a madam, and the shows and rich men involved only illicit transactions of sex for money.

Alfred Adams Jr.'s bathhouse had been in business since the late 1880s, and it provided lifeguards for its customers until the 1930s. It had checked in two million dollars worth of valuables, and not one cent had been stolen. The same could not be said, however, for the bathing suits that women purloined under their street clothes. Today, one cannot imagine slipping into a bathing suit that had been worn by hundreds of bathers. Just as appalling is the notion that one would want to keep such a garment.

During that bygone era, Adams' Bathhouse rented swimsuits for one dollar, and fashion-conscious women rejected the styles of previous years. After all, they sojourned on the Naughty Queen's island to be seen on the beach, reveal their figures, sun themselves until their bodies glowed, and indulge in summertime romances.

Tourists and islanders considered the ocean a hygienic pool, and parents with ailing children were advised by their physicians to take their youngsters with polio, asthma and whooping cough to the shore, where they could inhale the fresh sea air and swim in the therapeutic waters. Eventually, two hospitals were established for youngsters, the Children's Seashore House in Atlantic City and the Betty Bacharach Home in Longport.

In the aftermath of a sizzling 1930s summer, the pressure continued on police to "stop the pollution" that was corrupting lives with gambling and drinking. The police chief vowed to break down doors wherever a suspicion of gambling or drinking existed. But islanders felt no need to move their operations underground because they knew the chief's hoopla was for the newspapers and those who decried the sins of the Naughty Queen.

On one cool autumn day, police raided an apartment on South Kentucky Avenue, where they expected to find craps being played. They arrested the cutmen, who determined the amount of money, or vigorish, that players would have to pay the house, and the stickmen, who ran the games and took their name from the L-shaped sticks they used to retrieve thrown dice. The cutmen and stickmen turned out to have empty pockets and "dry mouths." The men had stashed the proceeds of their illegal activities into hidden compartments beneath the floor, and then covered the "traps" with rugs. Ultimately, the police confiscated a mere forty-five cents, which they returned to the men. Periodic raids such as that one portrayed police and city officials as leaders who were performing their civic duty, and the evangelists praised them for their "courage."

In truth, the raids were just for show because the police were controlled by Nucky, and he was tipped off whenever such "unscheduled" visits were to occur. But raids now and then made it look to the federal government that the Naughty Queen was cleaning her house and chasing the gangsters, pickpockets, prostitutes and other undesirables out of town.

When the brouhaha died down, the Naughty Queen's subjects resumed their illegal activities. The Queen smiled with contentment, relishing the jingle of money in her ample pockets.

By the late twenties, most horse-drawn carriages had given way to motorized cars along Atlantic Avenue. The common stench of manure had diminished greatly, though fishmongers still sold their goods from horse-drawn wagons, and fish smells still permeated the air. The icemen also still delivered blocks of ice from wagons.

When the Great Depression gripped the country, the Naughty Queen became a haven for the destitute. Unemployed men sought jobs as bellhops and waiters, women as maids and waitresses, in the grand Marlborough-Blenheim (which resembled a Moorish castle), Breakers, Chalfonte-Haddon Hall, St. Charles, Ambassador, Ritz-Carlton, Shelburne, Traymore, Dennis and Claridge hotels. They also sought positions in the smaller side-street hotels.

Tourists spent frugally, and islanders struggled, but Nucky's role as boss, and county treasurer, continued. Under his aegis, Atlantic County issued scrip bearing his signature. The certificates of varied face value could be used to make purchases in the county, but they could not be used as cash. Nucky himself had plenty of cash saved from his gambling and prostitution rackets, and now he also had his name, if not his hand, in islanders' pockets.

Nucky claimed islanders did not suffer as the rest of the country did during the Great Depression. He said no one went without food or coal, which was true. He and Lew Hermann, a friend and a journalist, raised two hundred thousand dollars for the needy, and the Queen's subjects praised the boss's leadership and compassion.

Nucky's own lifestyle had not been affected; his *joie de vivre* was ingrained in his personality, and due to his illegal profits over the years, he could afford the Depression. He often spent time in New York with the city's Mayor Jimmy Walker, a Democrat no less, and a friend who advised him to dip celery sticks in his champagne to avoid flatulence.

Back home, Atlantic City was gaining a reputation as a place that held bizarre wonders. An entrepreneur named Frank P. Gravatt owned the Steel Pier. There he featured acts such as the famous diving horses, upon whose magnificent backs beautiful young women rode as they leaped from great heights into the ocean. Gravatt also offered carnival acts that included boxing cats, Primo Carnero boxing with a kangaroo, for which Carnero received the sum of sixteen thousand dollars, to be divided among managers and trainers, and a man dancing with a tiger. The stars who could be seen glistening on the silver screen in Atlantic City included Shirley Temple, Paul Muni in *Scarface*, Carole Lombard, Clark Gable and William Powell.

Onstage, the performers included singer Dennis Day, Jack Haley, the Three Stooges and John Philip Sousa and his band. Sammy Kaye and his orchestra performed for dancers in ballrooms, and other big bands, including Glenn Miller and his orchestra, followed.

The Garden Pier featured the Emmett Welch Minstrels with Happy Thompson, whose real name was Martin Motz. Thompson, a happy-go-lucky sort of man, was born in Philadelphia, spent his childhood with a beloved aunt and adopted her last name of Thompson for his stage name. As a youngster, he stood upon a box and sang in the streets. He later joined a performing group called the "Cinamon Buns."

At age fifteen, he became part of the "Melody Monarchs" and took the name Happy Thompson. His voice deepened, and with his love of Emerald Isle melodies, he earned a reputation as the "Irish Tenor."

Thompson enlisted in the United States Army in 1917 and subsequently suffered an eye injury when a soldier threw a hand grenade at him in Germany. He was sent home, and his eyesight gradually worsened.

Emmett Welch hired Thompson for his minstrel show some still recall on Garden Pier, which now houses the Atlantic City Historical Museum. Despite his failing sight, Thompson never wavered in his up-beat attitude. He sang for the sheer joy of pleasing his audience and often stated that "If people applaud, you've earned it."

Thompson was blind by 1921, yet he did not so much as scowl about his loss. He sang at the Million Dollar Pier when the Emmett Welch Min-strels moved to Young's Hippodrome. Welch made him the featured solo-ist, and Thompson stayed with the minstrels for twenty years. He married a beautiful girl, Matilda Tracy, of the prominent Philadelphia family, and performed in that city as well as Atlantic City. While playing Dumont's, at Ninth and Arch streets, Thompson mastered his stage movements from every angle, and no one even suspected he was blind.

In the 1940s, Thompson sang at downtown Philadelphia cafes, and in the 1950s, he performed in Atlantic City at McDonough's Erin Café. He also directed the annual minstrel shows at Our Lady Star of the Sea Church at California and Atlantic avenues. In 1953, he appeared on a television show out of New York called *Open House*, and he spoke about the history of the Emmett Welch Minstrels.

Thompson always had a smile on his face, and a lilt to his voice. He died in 1955, leaving his wife, two children and four grandchildren. Matilda died in 1977.

Another Boardwalk feature of note was the Apollo Theatre, where the *Follies Bergere* was a featured show. The Globe Theatre, also on the boards, had the "cutie nudies" show, and Captain John Lake Young offered an aquarium, children's carnival, vaudeville acts, concerts and the latest rides at his Million Dollar Pier. There also was a dance floor there with burnished wood, which allowed dancers to glide across it.

But for Nucky, Atlantic City was wine, women and nightclubs. He assisted in creating what was known as the "World's Famous Playground," and he proudly showed it off each time he strolled the Boardwalk with an entourage of important politicians or other dignitaries. The bevy of beauties from his "harem" delighted his guests as well. He concluded, perhaps not incorrectly, that every desire or whim could be satisfied in his fair city.

Despite Nucky's hedonistic lifestyle, he was a religious man. He frequently attended Mass at Our Lady Star of the Sea Church, where he would sit in a rear pew, and he dropped sizable donations in the collection basket. One can only imagine that he departed with an uplifted spirit. Sometimes, he told John Stoneburg, the author of an unpublished biography of Nucky, he even sought solitude and respite on retreats to a monastery.

Nucky's creatively entrepreneurial mind did not end with the colossal Convention Hall. He thought, and it may seem obvious given his penchant for women, that the spectacle of a beauty contest after Labor Day would be just the thing to extend the tourist season, and spending, by a week.

Stoneburg wrote that Nucky consulted with Mayor Bader, who agreed that bathing beauties gracing a parade of wicker rolling chairs on the Boardwalk could only help the city. Different accounts of the first Miss America Pageant credit local hotelmen with proposing the idea of wicker rolling chairs, a conveyance unique to Atlantic City, parading along the Boardwalk. In those accounts, the 1921 beauty contest is incidental to the parade itself. And in truth, unlike today's megapageant in which thousands vie for the single job, only eight contestants competed that year. Sixteen-year-old Margaret Gorman, from Washington, D.C., won.

Nucky arranged for showgirls from the *Follies Bergere, George White's Scandals* and Earl Carroll's *Vanities* to participate in the parade. Stoneburg said that Nucky purchased a beautiful costume for Evelyn Nesbit to wear in the contest. Nesbit, sans her red-velvet swing, contrived to be perched above all the other beauties. But she had consumed perhaps a bit too much gin, and when she threw kisses to the crowd, she tripped and rolled onto the Boardwalk. When she got up, she looked a mess, and her gown was plastered with horse dung.

Nucky was humiliated and livid, and he revealed a side of himself that was not often seen.

"Louie, pick up the bitch, brush her off, and when the parade is over, tell here to get out of my city, and never come back again!" he bellowed in one breath.

"Sure, Boss," Louie replied.

Later that evening, Nucky entertained guests in his suite at the Ritz-Carlton. Among those attending his party were Jimmy Walker and Johnny D'Agostino, Nucky's best friend. Johnny's family owned Renault Winery, located about 18 miles west of Atlantic City in Egg Harbor City. The winery still is in operation today, although it is owned by a different family.

In another suite at the Ritz-Carlton, a young woman also was holding court. She was Marion Davies, an actress adored by millions in general and by newspaper publisher William Randolph Hearst in particular.

According to Stoneburg's biography of Nucky, some people believed that Nucky had insulted Davies and called her a tramp. Others said that Nucky's friend Joe Moss, who operated the Silver Slipper Supper Club with Nucky, had tried to woo her. Whatever the truth, she left the Naughty Queen in a huff and returned to California, where she related her vexation to Hearst, a titan of the Fourth Estate.

Rumors followed that an enraged Hearst journeyed to Atlantic City but left without any noticeable encounter.

Yet another account holds that Hearst already was in Atlantic City with Davies when the offending incident occurred. Carlo M. Sardella, in an *Atlantic City Press* article, "The Night the Red Lights Went Out in Atlantic City," wrote that Hearst and Davies were dressed to the nines one night at Babette's Yacht Bar. They were planning an evening of fun, but they encountered a cross Nucky instead. Nucky's unmistakable voice rang out across the room as he supposedly made some vicious comments about Davies.

Whichever story is true, Nucky made a powerful enemy of a man with a lot of ink and a sensational bent that felt no obligation to the truth. And Hearst used more than a little of his ink to write about Nucky's Atlantic City: A Hearst archive, the New York Journal-American Newspaper Morgue in Austin, Texas, holds substantial files on the Naughty Queen and her boss.

For his part, Nucky remained secluded with his friends, telling them with bravado: "He's a windbag who a dumb broad has played for a sucker. He's printing lies about me. Let the matter rest, the old bastard may come back as a ghost to haunt me."

Despite Nucky's seeming indifference to the matter, a pall hung over him. William Randolph Hearst's name signified great power. But, Nucky also was a powerful man with connections among senators and congressmen.

Now autumn leaves denuded trees. Some days the ocean was subdued, on others , it churned from seasonal storms. On days when the warm breezes still blew, islanders came en masse to the Boardwalk. Nucky often stood at the railing of the Boardwalk, where he was mesmerized by the ocean's beauty and inhaled the salty air that made him feel so alive. He would stroll the boards, greeting merchants and asking about their well-being. Then he would turn down Tennessee Avenue, enter a bar, and order a drink as the player piano blared, "Ev'ry little breeze seems to whisper Louise ... birds in the trees seem to whisper Louise. Can it be true, someone like you can love me?"

When he was finished, Nucky thanked the owner, whose name was Louise, and shook hands with the customers who surrounded him. As dusk cloaked the skies, Nucky returned to the Boardwalk. Neon signs swayed to the tune of chilly winds and glittered for the pleasure of any who saw them. The wind god, Aeolus, prodded cumulus clouds out to sea, and Nucky turned up his collar, returning home with a contented smile upon his face.

The repeal of Prohibition in 1933 enabled islanders to obtain liquor licenses without a problem. Once again, evangelists complained to city fathers about excessive gambling and drinking. The city fathers complied with their concerns by reducing liquor licenses from one hundred seventy-seven to one hundred fifty-six.

The freedom to do whatever one wanted was intrinsic to the Naughty Queen's personality. The constant parade of earnest do-gooders equaled the zeal of the *bons vivants*, who unabashedly asserted their live-and-let-live philosophy.

The repeal of Prohibition, while generally welcomed, had created a small, unforeseen problem — there was a lack of proper glasses for cocktails. Consequently, Christmas presents consisted of decanters, glassware for old-fashioneds, manhattans and martinis and crystal stemware for champagne. Restaurants, nightclubs and cafes redecorated with mirrors and glass. The Queen saw her reflected image and smiled.

At the Colton Manor Hotel on South Pennsylvania Avenue, dinner cost eighty-five cents, and drinks were thirty-five cents to fifty cents. Tourists complained about the outrageous prices, but they also consoled themselves because they were in the World's Famous Playground, where one expected to play and pay for the pleasure.

During that time, the Steel Pier featured Paul Muni in *Scarface*, and Sammy Kaye and his orchestra played for one thousand romantics in the pier's ballroom. The beautiful Sonora, a courageous girl and excellent swimmer, dived by day on the back of a horse from forty feet in the air into the ocean. After several years of diving, Sonora suffered detached retinas and lost her eyesight. Only those close to her knew that she was blind. There was a rumor that the horses suffered the same fate, but it was never proved.

Nucky welcomed many a star to perform in Atlantic City. The first all-black Broadway show previewed in Atlantic City when, in the twenties, Eubie Blake and Noble Sissle performed *Shuffle Along* at the Apollo with Josephine Baker. A dancer and actor named Georgie Raft took the stage at The Silver Slipper before becoming George Raft. His suave manner, romantic dancing and mode of dress were emulated throughout nightclubs and cafes on the island.

The Naughty Queen beamed with her new prosperity. Despite the repeal of Prohibition, bootleggers still purchased Canadian whiskey for eight dollars a pint. The mayor, Harry Bacharach, warned cafe owners they could be penalized for purchasing bootleg whiskey, and he chided tourists for their aberrant behavior.

"I know people who are saints at home, but in Atlantic City, they seek risque places," the mayor said. "The behavior of the customer is important because the state will control the number of liquor licenses, rather than allowing municipalities the control."

One morning when islanders opened their businesses, they found their slot machines had been stolen. Even though gambling was illegal, the thefts were reported, and police detectives were assigned to "the case of the missing slots." They searched for the thieves, but made no arrests, discovering only that two gangs of two-armed bandits had made off with the machines. Police expressed surprise, however, to find that there were eighty-seven slot machines in a one-block radius.

People thought crackdowns now would be inevitable, but Police Chief George Leeds gave them some good news: "Since the repeal of Prohibition, the city has further advantages," he said. "There will be less work for the police department in this era with a scarcity of souses."

But an editorial in the *Atlantic City Daily Press* enraged islanders, whose survival depended on illegal activities:

> Criminals are as bloodthirsty and barbaric as any Sioux or Blackfoot braves of the Sitting Bull era. The death penalty is barbaric, but life imprisonment may be a more 'exquisitely' barbarous torture than a few minutes in a lethal chamber or at the end of a rope. Lifelong incarceration on some inaccessible and unprepossessing 'devil's island' may cause a fall-off in crime.

And yet, new nightclubs sprang up throughout the city with cathouses above the premises. There was Mike Healy's Palm Room at the Clicquot Club, located on North Illinois Avenue, and Eddie Kravis's Paddock International at the corner of Illinois and Atlantic avenues. Most of the clubs were "bust-out joints" for conventioneers who released their inhibitions as they experienced everything and anything available to them.

Was there something in the air that caused such aberrant behavior? Or was it knowing you could indulge your personal desires without shame? Perhaps it was a catharsis from life's daily struggles. Whatever it was, tourists unleashed their fantasies in the bawdiness of the Naughty Queen's island.

A kind of peace reigned among different factions in the city under Boss Nucky. Occasionally, fights broke out, but killings were rare. One of Nucky's henchmen was discovered hanging from his basement pipes. Police ruled out suicide, but the killer never was found. Another time, a man escaped death when a bullet aimed at him landed in the side of the Apollo Theatre instead. But all in all, the island was rather peaceful.

It was business as usual in the Naughty Queen. Meanwhile, clubs offered roulette, faro, poker, craps and *chemin de fer*. Payoffs greased politicians' hands, and they, in turn, spread their graft with a hundred-dollar C-note here, and half a C-note there.

On the north side of Kentucky Avenue, Club Harlem featured Count Basie and his orchestra with a bevy of tall, beautiful black girls dancing in a revue. Larry Steele, the highly respected master of ceremonies, returned to Club Harlem every summer, and the club's fame spread throughout the land.

The *Will Mastin Trio*, starring singer and dancer Sammy Davis Jr., appeared at Club Harlem. Sammy's mother, Elvera, also known as "Baby Sanchez," worked as a bartender at Grace's Little Belmont across the street.

Club Harlem has since closed, and despite current public support for such a night spot, it is not likely to open again. The original building was torn down and replaced by a parking lot. But the club lives on through its history. A man named Willie Gainer displays relics from Club Harlem at a Kentucky Avenue museum, where jazz sessions also are performed.

The battle of the titans had begun. William Randolph Hearst's campaign against Nucky appeared to be relentless through the publisher's powerful weapons: newspapers that reported on Nucky's illegal operations, and on the city leaders who allowed such dealings. Hearst did not realize that Nucky, who had the tongue of an orator, was the champion of his people. Nucky had tremendous energy, even if it did seem to be time-released. He once asked of his friend Mayor Walker: "How can a man be so tired all day long and come to life after the sun goes down, and the burgundy flows as red as blood into his gullet?"

"I guess you're a night person," Walker replied.

"Yes, I am."

He was peculiarly fastidious, too.

After conducting some business with cohorts, Nucky welcomed a ravishing redhead with hair down to her waist to his cottage. He embraced her, and she asked if she could use the bathroom.

"Sure, use all the facilities," he said casually.

"What does that mean?"

"Take a bath, Doll, take a bath."

She giggled. Nucky was known for his penchant for cleanliness.

One of Nucky's favorite hangouts was the ship-shaped Babette's Yacht Bar at Mississippi and Pacific avenues. Babette, whose given name was Blanche, and who previously had performed under the stage name of Blanche Babbitt, was the lovely and willowy wife of owner Dan Stebbins. In his younger days, during Prohibition, Stebbins had been the proprietor of speakeasies. Babette was not a procuress in the worst sense of the word, but she did provide beauties to adorn Nucky's parties.

During the summer, she and Dan entertained dignitaries on their forty-foot yacht. In the winter, she strolled the Boardwalk in her full-length chinchilla coat and hat.

Nucky's best friend, Johnny D'Agostino, usually met Nucky at Babette's. Johnny was a handsome man with flashing dark eyes, and he also was wealthy. His ancestors were said to have included European counts and cardinals of the Roman Catholic Church. At Babette's, Johnny and Nucky ran a tab as they drank champagne. Naturally, bartenders padded the bill, but they should have known better. No one could fool Nucky. Once after he and Johnny had drunk their fill of the bubbly beverage, Nucky counted the corks. The bartender hung his head, embarrassed, and he apologized.

Another time, Dan Stebbins walked over to Nucky and whispered to him:

"Have you heard about Al Brown?"

Nucky scratched his balding head and tugged at his ear. He was perplexed.

"Who is he ... politician or gangster?"

"I don't know," Stebbins answered. "I met one of the Fetter boys at the Ambassador Hotel, and he told me Brown had a three-room suite at the Jefferson Hotel. They say girls are coming by the busloads."

"He must be a gangster or politician," Nucky reasoned. "Who else could have that kind of money?"

He was a gangster as it turned out: "Al Brown" was the notorious Al Capone.

Nucky claimed he did not know Capone, but they were photographed together at a 1929 gangster convention. Nucky claimed that the Hearst newspaper the *New York Journal* had superimposed a photograph of him onto the Capone shot. Nucky defensively noted that he was wearing a summer suit in the photograph, while Capone wore winter clothes.

And now snow blanketed the island, marquee lights glittered, and the city resembled a fairyland. Nucky had spent Christmas Eve delivering baskets of food to the needy, politely brushing aside their gratitude, and enjoying their happy faces. He spent Christmas alone, reflecting upon the day, and enjoying the solitude and respite from his hectic life.

New Year's Eve had the opposite effect on Nucky. He invited two hundred guests to the Ritz-Carlton Hotel for a trademark night of revelry. The men and women wore tuxedos and gowns, and his own tux was accented by his ever-present carnation boutonniere. White-gloved waiters kept food, liquor and champagne flowing through the reception hall. It was a glorious evening, a pinnacle of elegance, after which things could only get worse.

And the next morning they did. Louie Kessel awoke Nucky at 8 o'clock in the morning.

"Louie, I just got to bed," Nucky protested. "What is it?"

"I'm sorry, Boss. There are guys snooping around. 'Big Lip' Louie called. He's seen tons of cameras, typing machines, and that ain't all."

"What else?"

"The Lip sees two of them in the Western Union. So he watches through the window, and they made the wire. Lip goes in, and snatches the pad they're using. He reads it and traces the message. Here ... read it":

Suggesting advancing deadline tomorrow. Everything is set on this end. Copy enroute by courier. Private line installed. Signed: Connors

Nucky leaped out of bed and put on his robe while Kessel ran his bath.

"Louie, did your friend find out where the wire was sent?"

"Oh yeah, Boss. The editor of the *New York Journal*."

"Hearst!" Nucky spat. "This is his work."

"Yeah, Boss."

"Louie, get some boys. I want you to cover every possible outlet, every newsstand in Atlantic City, Pleasantville, Ventnor and Margate. Put an advance order for the *Journal*. I don't know what those dudes are up to, but we'll play it safe until I find out."

"Boss, what do you want I should do with all those papers?'

"Bring me a copy, then make a bonfire and burn the rest."

Were the Naughty Queen and the Boss about to be burned themselves?

Kessel and the boys met the speedy Nellie Bly mail train — named for the famous reporter who had circled the Earth in 72 days — placed the newspapers in trucks, drove to the city dump and had their bonfire. Kessel returned to Nucky and handed him the single newspaper, which Nucky unfolded to read:

Atlantic City Vice Exposed

The point size of the headline was big enough to make the exasperated Nucky exclaim: "My God, he's using the type they save for the end of the world!"

"It's bad, Boss."

"It isn't good," retorted Nucky.

"Boss, you want I should get some boys and croak those snoops?"

"No, I want to be left alone. Call Johnny, tell him it's serious."

"Are you sure you burned all those newspapers?"

"Yeah, Boss, they're burned."

Kessel dialed Johnny D'Agostino's number and handed the telephone to Nucky, who read the headline and the decks beneath it to Johnny:

Rum, Dope, Gambling Rings In Control
Probe Reveals White Slave Gang Kidnapping School Girls

Nucky shook his head in disgust and continued:

Atlantic City's playground of millionaires has been taken over, lock, stock and barrel. Al Capone is one of its ring leaders. Gangsters roam the streets unmolested, assaulting, ravishing and murdering at will with no fear of punishment.

"He's a madman!" Nucky yelled.

In actuality, Atlantic City was rather safe. It was a wonderful place to raise children, who could walk about the city without fear. Their parents strolled the city streets and Boardwalk at night without a thought to their safety. Even the poorest families enjoyed the beach and ocean like wealthy tourists, and hot dog roasts were often held safely on the beach at night.

Johnny D'Agostino arrived and read the newspaper.

"Nuck," he said, "that guy has some imagination. Maybe we should get out of town?"

"Are you serious?" Nucky replied in disbelief. "Listen to this ... 'In manpower, guile, ruthlessness, a wealthy rum-gambling underworld constitutes the largest enemy ever pitted against the United States ...' my name isn't mentioned, but everyone knows he means me."

"Nuck, old man Hearst is as smart as he is vindictive," D'Agostino said. "If that garbage is an example of his wisdom, I wouldn't let it bother you."

But Nucky was bothered.

"Johnny," he said, "this is a campaign against me ... no flash in the pan."

Florence Osbeck, who preferred to be called Flossie, lived in Philadelphia but frequently came to Atlantic City. She was a tall, stunning blonde who had won a cash prize at Nucky's Silver Slipper Supper Club for being the best-looking girl. The evening she won, Nucky had been out of town. But Flossie had as much verve as Nucky, and it was destined that they should one day meet.

She called her girlfriend, the red-haired Hazel Scott.

"Feel like some salt air tonight?"

"Sure, Flossie," Scott responded. "What's going on?"

"There's a party at the Ritz-Carlton, and they're paying girls to attend. Mickey Duffy said we can use his room for the night."

"In Atlantic City?" Hazel asked.

"No place else. Hurry, let's get the show on the road."

Flossie was a friend of Duffy's, a first-class "stillman" who made his own booze. He also had big, black cars that he used for his tour business to Atlantic City.

Flossie and Hazel arrived in Atlantic City and took an elevator to the reception room, where a gala event was in evidence. The two damsels from the City of Brotherly Love slithered into the mix. Then Flossie grasped her friend's arm.

"Look!" she said, pointing to a table at which a gnomelike man with a hook nose hunched over a stack of greenbacks. He did not look up once as he continued to hand out hundred-dollar bills.

"My God, that monkey's passing out C-notes like there ain't no tomorrow!" Flossie exclaimed.

The women stood in line, and when they reached the man, he handed each of them a crisp one-hundred-dollar bill.

"Hazel, do you see what I see? He doesn't even look up," Flossie said. "Let's get in line again."

"No, I'm afraid," Hazel said.

"This is real sticky; watch me," Flossie said. She giggled and returned to the money man again, and again. Still, he never looked up. But another man standing in the doorway was watching. He nodded to Lou Holtz, a man whom Flossie knew slightly. Lou put his hand on Flossie's arm.

"Look, Doll," he said, "you're not playing the game straight. Give the money back to the nice man.'

"Take your filthy paws off me!" Flossie shouted with desperate indignation.

Nearby tables were laden with fresh fruit, and Flossie grabbed a McIntosh apple, which she hurled at Lou, who jumped aside. The man behind him took the full impact of the fruit on his genitals. Groaning, he bent over and fell to the floor.

"My God, Flossie, you killed him," Lou exclaimed. "You killed Al Jolson."

"Good, now he can sing with the angels. C'mon, Hazel, let's get out of here!" Flossie grabbed Hazel's hand, they ran to the elevator, and they didn't stop until they reached their room.

Guests ran to the scene of the "crime" and hovered over Jolson. A beefy man with a sinister-looking scar running down his cheek demanded to know who had caused Jolson's injury.

"Mr. Brown, some broad hit him below in his privates ... that blonde ... say, where is she?"

Upstairs in their room, terror raced through Flossie and Hazel. Their hearts pounded. They came up with a plan, placed the bureau behind the door and heaved a sigh of relief. But Flossie had attended enough parties at the Ritz-Carlton that she was known to the staff, and that was about to become a problem.

Suddenly, there was pounding on the door. Flossie and Hazel jumped in renewed fear.

"Open up, Flossie," a man called out. "Mr. Brown wants to see you."

"Tell him to fly a kite," Flossie shot back with bravado.

"Oh no, Flossie, that guy with the ugly scar is Al Capone," Hazel said.

Flossie pursed her lips, and placed her hands on her hips.

"Hazel, I don't care. He can still go fly a kite," she said. She paced the floor and pondered her next move.

"If we were in Philly, I'd call Mickey Duffy."

"Wait, Flossie. I have an idea. Do you know Nucky Johnson?"

"Sure, everybody does. Let's send him a message with a carrier pigeon with an SOS."

"Stop joking! If Jolson is dead ..."

Hazel's hand trembled as she dialed the operator and placed a call to Nucky's cottage.

"Who is this?" a gruff voice asked.

"Nucky, my name is Hazel Scott. I met you at the Beaux Arts with Joe Moss. My friend and I are in deep trouble."

"Tell me about it."

Hazel related the events leading to Al Jolson's injury. When she was done, Nucky asked for her room number. She told him "five sixteen."

"I'll be right there," he said.

Now the pounding on the door resumed, with yelling: "Open up, in the name of the law!"

Oh no, the police were involved! But the next thing Flossie and Hazel knew, a booming voice halted the pounding.

"What are you bastards doing to my hotel?" the new voice hollered as its owner winked at the officers. Then, gently, "Girls, open the door."

Flossie and Hazel pushed the bureau away and opened the door to a multitude of glaring faces.

"Hazel, good to see you," Nucky said cordially. "Miss, pleased to meet you. What's your name?"

"Flossie Osbeck. I won the contest last month at your club."

"Sorry, I wasn't there. The judges made a good choice," Nucky said. "Listen, those guys were having fun with you."

"You mean, Jolson isn't dead?" Flossie asked.

"Naw, he's a little sore. He's with Peaches Browning in the hall. I just saw him."

"Mr. Johnson, thanks a lot."

"Flossie, call me 'Nuck.'"

She smiled, relieved, and unaware at that moment that she had just met her future husband, a man whom she would be calling "Nuck" for a very long time.

The next day, Nucky strolled the Boardwalk. The sun glistened on the ocean, resembling millions of tiny diamonds. As he returned to his cottage, he encountered a woman named Vivian. Nucky had known her for a couple of years.

Vivian was beautifully groomed, and a large, picture hat framed her face. She held the arm of a man with an ugly scar on his face: Al Capone.

An interesting moment ensued, during which the two men, who clearly knew each other, pretended to be strangers. Vivian introduced them — "Mr. Brown, meet Mr. Johnson" — and they exchanged pleasantries.

No one knew why Al Capone used the name Brown; after all, his face revealed his identity.

"Mr. Brown, a pleasure."

When Capone and Vivian continued on their way, Nucky shook his head.

"What's a classy girl like Vivian doing with Al Capone?" he wondered.

Meanwhile, the Hearst newspapers were unrelenting, reporting that Al Capone visited Atlantic City frequently. Nucky denied that, stating, "He visited Atlantic City for one week."

After Capone's visit to Atlantic City, he went to Philadelphia, where he was arrested on a weapons charge. He spent an unscheduled visit in Cell 63 of the Holmesburg prison.

Atlantic City attracted Al Capone, and his news value attracted Hearst. The city was "good copy," and Hearst wasn't about to miss one single-copy sale. His *New York Journal* reported:

From the warm, broad, white beaches with its leisurely breakers with rambling piers, Atlantic City resembles some fantastic fairyland with a skyline of gargantuan, weirdly-designed hotels, soaring above the board-walk. Vice and degeneracy are rampant to a degree seldom exceeded in human history. The orgies and perversions described by Suetonius, historian from 75 to 150 A.D., and Petronius, satirist, who died in 66 A.D., equal and describe the Roman decadence revealed by the fantastic and incredibly corrupt acts of degeneracy offered to convention delegates that enter the city.

Johnny D'Agostino shook his head as he read the article.

"That ought to get your convention bureau some business," he observed. Nucky nodded.

On January 4, 1930, the *New York Journal* headlines again blazed:

Vice Lord Rules Atlantic City!
Fear Keeps Up Flow Of Graft Money

The article stated:

He (Nucky) has entertained ambassadors, governors, senators, "Scarface" Capone with such magic powers by his lavish spending, and with his "Hatchet Man" Cappy Hoffman who puffs on his opium pipe and "soars" into the night, with shots heard on dark streets, and bodies in a distant ditch. He's arrested, his dope outfit is seized as well as his two guns. The hatchet man grins, it's not a pleasant sight. Soon he's freed on bail, being a hatchet man is fun and has little danger.

And then, two days later, on January 6, 1930:

Atlantic City's Hatchet Man is Samuel "Cappy" Hoffman, a member of Max "Boo-boo's," Huff's Philadelphia gang, loaned to Atlantic City's Vice-Lord to see that there is honor among thieves. Cappy Hoffman is allowed to declare himself in any racket in the city. He also operates his own "house of shame."

Nucky said: "It's time to round up the boys."

Calls went out to Atlantic City Mayor Anthony Ruffu Jr., Judge

Joseph Anthony Corio, Police Chief Patrick Doran, Councilman William Cuthbert and Chief of County Detectives Frank Harrold.

"You've seen what the Hearst's newspapers have to say about Atlantic City," Nucky said. "It's time for action. I want a few places closed down and arrests made."

According to *The Atlantic Reporter*, which contains extensive records of court actions from several states, including New Jersey, detectives raided Cappy Hoffman's apartment on November 30, 1929. Hoffman was at home, asleep in a back bedroom. His pal, Toufeek "Too'fick" Baroody, was asleep with his seventeen-year-old mistress, Josephine, in the front of the apartment.

Police found several burners, a handful of spoons, some needles and an old coffee tin containing "yen-shee," or opium ashes. The officers also found two loaded revolvers. Too'fick and his mistress were arrested on narcotics charges. When she was asked her name, the girl replied:

"Missus Baroody."

"You're married to this thug?"

"Watch your language, Copper. I'll get your badge. D'is is my wife, like she said, and we're married in d'sight of God."

"Sergeant, take them away ... separate cells."

Hoffman was awakened by the commotion of the detectives questioning Too'fick. Cappy came into the hall to find the detective holding the tin of opium residue and said, "What do you want that for? Give us a break."

They didn't.

When Cappy was brought into the courtroom, he was shaken by the sight of his wife, Florence Williams Hoffman, who also had been arraigned on a narcotics charge. The trial took place in Mays Landing, and the curious crowded the courtroom. Cappy was convicted and sentenced on February 28, 1930, to seven years at Trenton State Prison. He also was fined two thousand dollars, real money any day and an especially large sum during the Great Depression. He paid his fine on September 20, 1932. On the same day, Cappy also was sentenced for gaming and bookmaking and received five consecutive years in prison and another fine, this time for five thousand dollars. As Cappy left the courtroom, he threatened to speed Judge William Smathers to his maker at the first opportunity.

Too'fick Baroody got seven years and a two thousand-dollar fine for possession of a controlled dangerous substance. Too'fick, like Cappy, was found guilty of gaming and bookmaking and received a three-year sentence and three thousand-dollar fine on top of the drug conviction. Cappy's wife and Too'fick's "missus" each got a three-year sentence at what is now known as the Edna Mahan Correctional Facility for Women in Clinton. When Florence heard her sentence, she shouted imprecations at Judge Smathers and was led away in a state of hysteria.

As Cappy, Florence, Too'fick and Josephine were brought into the system and charges were investigated and proved, the Atlantic County investigators showed they were not impotent — as long as they were given the go-ahead by Nucky Johnson.

The commotion had died down, and Nucky went to Babette's Yacht Bar, where he joined Babette and Dan. According to Stoneburg's account, Babette played the femme fatale and flirted with Nucky, which disturbed her husband. When Dan excused himself, Babette told Nucky he had suppressed his desire for her. Nucky told her she was a dreamer. Although he could have just about any woman he wanted, she was not on his list.

"Anyone who picks on a married woman is a damn fool," he said. "Men will play with you, and where's the percentage with all the loose women around?"

Soon Nucky had a bigger problem than Babette Stebbins. It was an old problem that kept coming back to him, one that also started with a woman, but that had since taken on a life of its own.

Nucky unfolded the *New York Journal* one afternoon while his maid prepared his customary breakfast of fresh orange juice, a dozen eggs and bacon, fresh rolls and coffee. He called out to Louie Kessel:

"Have you read this?'

"Yeah, Boss."

Party Boss Denies Affiliation With Capone

"Boss, Capone gives me the creeps," Louie confided, "killing all those babies."

"What babies?" Nucky asked.

"Boss, some geezer told me he shot those moron babies with machine guns and used them as valentines."

"Louie, that's ridiculous," Nucky scoffed. "Such lies."

In the centerfold of another newspaper, there was an article about Hearst and Nucky:

> Under different circumstances, Hearst and Nucky Johnson might have been friends. Hearst considers Nucky of little intelligence, but Hearst is wrong. Nucky's intelligence equals or surpasses Hearst, but Nucky is not a vindictive man like Hearst.

Nucky smiled. He was pleased to read something favorable about himself.

Late in the afternoon, Nucky strolled the Boardwalk with Louie. Nucky gazed at the rough ocean, becoming introspective about his life as a feeling of loneliness overcame him.

"Louie, when you're at the top, there is no one to turn to but God, and too many are strangers to His name. What a terrible thing it would be, to be president of the United States ... so alone."

"Boss, I'm here."

"Thanks, Louie."

The next morning, Louie shook Nucky.

"Boss, wake up. The joint is crawling with Feds."

"What joint? The city? Pack my bags. I'm leaving."

"But where?"

"I'll tell you. Pick up Eve, or rather, Evan Fontaine."

"Sounds like a man's name. Boss, shouldn't you hang around?"

"She's a lady. No, a man needs respite from his problems. Drive me to Hammonton. We're going to stay at Charlie's Motel."

Nucky and Evan Fontaine spent two days and nights in Charlie's Motel. They ordered their meals and made love day and night. Nucky found peace in the arms of the beautiful woman.

On the third day, Louie knocked on the door.

"Boss! The whole town's on fire!"

"Give me a fiddle, and I'll follow the wake of history," the re-energized Nucky said. "Please do not disturb m'lady before noon. Tell her I shall return in the cool of the evening, when the time is right for love-making."

Nucky went back to Atlantic City and called upon the police department.

"I understand there are a lot of 'foreign' law enforcements in town. Any truth to it?"

"Yes, Nuck. They moved in last night. Special agents from the Justice and Treasury departments. Three of the men from the Treasury Department are in the mayor's office. Any orders, Boss?"

"Not that I can think of," Nucky replied. "Let me know the minute you hear anything."

The following day, there was another Nucky story in the *New York Journal*:

Nucky Johnson Oppresses Colored People

Atlantic City's blacks were infuriated with the headline and sent a statement to the *Journal* criticizing its accusation. The letter stated: "We say Nucky is our leader. He does more for the Negro people every day."

Nucky was uplifted when he read the statement. He shook hands with his friends, feeling relief and joy. When he was alone again, he strolled the Boardwalk and surveyed his city. His life's work had brought with it feelings of both unbridled ecstasy and tremendous weight. Nucky met up with a friend and told him, "Don't ever get to be boss. It's awful. I give people what they want — whiskey, wine, women, song and slot machines. I don't deny it or apologize for it."

Now reporters stormed the city, and Nucky entertained many of them at the Ritz-Carlton Hotel, hoping for favorable publicity. Even

H.L. Mencken and Theodore Dreiser visited him. Dreiser gave him a copy of his latest book, *An American Tragedy*.

Nucky's lust for life strengthened him amid the Hearst attacks. The newspaper baron's vitriolic statements in print no longer fazed him. He laughed, walked bareheaded in the sun and relished his Boardwalk and the temperamental ocean.

The offshore action was tempestuous, too. Nucky and Flossie had dated since their first meeting in the mid-thirties. But both were passionate people, and that made for bitter arguments. One thing they argued about was the one thing Nucky was not ready to give Flossie: Marriage.

"Nucky, why don't you make me an honest woman?" Flossie asked at one point.

"Flossie," he said grinning, "I didn't know you were dishonest."

Almost fifteen million tourists now visited Atlantic City every summer. The city had more than three hundred hotels, twenty thousand rooms and four miles of stores and restaurants on the Boardwalk.

Nucky reminisced with friends about the old days, when the idea of a Convention Hall had been called a folly and when he had invited Jersey City's mayor to his club, when Eleanor Powell, Jimmy Durante, Irving Berlin and Norma Talmadge were his guests. Frank Hague had refused to support Nucky's endeavors.

"I won't do anything to stop you, but it's your funeral," Hague said bluntly. Just as pointedly, he wanted to know about that photo of Nucky and Al Capone.

"That fake picture did me more harm than good," Nucky railed. "I never walked with Capone. I told people that the *New York Journal's* photographer superimposed two photographs. If you noticed, I had a summer suit on, while Capone and his crony had on winter clothes."

There was no question that the Naughty Queen had adored Nucky. She had showered him with wealth, and power, and all that went with his anointed position. But the Queen became restless. She was even a bit bored, and she began to yearn for someone new and exciting, vivacious and — bless her — young.

There were many ambitious men who were willing to step into Nucky's favored position. The Queen would choose two men this time, one a politician, the other a flamboyant, charismatic and street-smart kid, born and bred in Atlantic City: Paul E. "Skinny" D'Amato.

Skinny was born on December 4, 1908. He was one of eight children born to Italian immigrant Emilio D'Amato and his Italian-American wife, Mary DiSanti D'Amato. Two brothers died as youngsters, leaving Skinny with one brother, Emil, born November 13, 1912, and known as Willie. The boys had four sisters, Marie, Rose, Columbia and Antoinette, who preferred to be called Patty.

The family resided in Atlantic City's Ducktown section, which is a five-block area from Missouri to Fairmount avenues. The neighborhood got its name from the ducks that occasionally waddled across the corduroy road at Florida and the bay and now and then ended up on a dinner table during the Depression. Italian-Americans found the name offensive back then, but it persists today, and even has been accorded a level of pride to the extent that there are plans for a Ducktown renaissance.

Skinny declared his independence at age ten, asserting his emancipation by running away from home and playing hooky from school. When he did go to school, the enterprising lad ran craps and card games in the school yard. When he did not go, he set up his gambling operations in vacant houses, on the train platform and on street corners. When Skinny would return home, his father punished him severely.

The cycle repeated itself as Emilio D'Amato was a harsh disciplinarian, and Skinny was never one to be told what to do. A natural leader and risk-taker, Skinny found his father's house and rules too confining. He ran away frequently. Willie knew all his brother's havens, and their mother sent him to Skinny's hideouts with fresh clothing and food.

Some mob figures also had local retreats. They stayed in Margate during the summer months, ordering in from Emilio's bar and restaurant. Skinny, who was thirteen years old, and Willie, who was nine, were dispatched by trolley to deliver the orders.

When Skinny was fourteen, his father died from a stroke. Emilio was thirty-eight years old, and, despite running a successful bar and restaurant, he left his family destitute. Emilio had bailed many islanders out of jail, and some had skipped out on it, leaving Emilio with liens on his business, and on his home.

With his father's death, Skinny moved out of his mother's house, and Willie assumed responsibility for supporting the family. He worked odd jobs, delivered orders for neighborhood grocers and looked after his younger sisters. When he was ten years old, he quit school so that he could work as a delivery boy for a meat market. His generous boss, John Capone (no relation to Al Capone), sent Willie home with meat and groceries for the family. At the end of the week, Willie handed his mother his unopened pay envelope.

After his father's death, Skinny applied for a construction job. He lied about his age, saying he was eighteen, and he was hired. One day, he was on a scaffold as fierce winds blew onshore from the ocean. Skinny momentarily lost his footing and was lucky not to lose more. From that day on, he decided he would make his living in a safer line of work: Gambling.

Now fifteen years old, Skinny borrowed forty-five dollars from an uncle. He rented a pool hall and sold trinkets, cigars and cigarettes for a penny apiece. In the rear of the poolroom, card and crap games went on day and night. At eleven years of age, Willie worked with him, learning how to deal.

Now six feet tall and extremely thin, Skinny was called the "dart," a name he detested. The neighborhood guys teased him out of affection, and admiration. Skinny was tall, about five-foot-eleven, and handsome, with dark hair, dark eyes, and an aquiline nose. He walked with a swagger, and a cigarette almost always dangled from the side of his mouth. In later years, he would smoke six packs of cigarettes a day, puncturing them so that he would not inhale all of the smoke. He would wash them down with forty cups of coffee.

Although Skinny was lanky, he was a strong and tough opponent. He was challenged routinely for his budding power base by people who envied, feared and respected him to varying degrees. The vanquished ultimately kow-towed to him because Skinny was a natural leader, able to coalesce others to do his bidding. By the age of sixteen, Skinny wore custom-made suits, and contrary to what has been said about him, he dressed conservatively. The only jewelry he ever wore was a watch.

By the time he was twenty, Skinny owned fifteen "horse joints" throughout Atlantic City, where men bet and played pool. He became known as the "master shuffler," mixing cards and people with equal skill. Johnny Biondi, a local bookmaker during the thirties and forties, said of Skinny: "He uses a 'lavender touch' on people. You don't have a chance. He can take off your pants before you realize what's happening."

Skinny's suave manner, appealing personality, generosity, and lavender touch, paid off for him. His friends stuck with him, and his enemies, the smart ones, became his friends. In both jest and tribute, his minions adopted an Arabic custom of greeting and departure, bowing and gesturing as they spoke, "Salaam, Allah-Skinn."

As Skinny grew older, his handsome looks, power and money became an aphrodisiac. Women sought him out and adored him; friends lived vicariously through him. His reputation soared. Whether he entered a restaurant, bar or nightclub, the Naughty Queen treated him as if he were royalty.

Skinny gained fame as a power broker and club owner, but he was something of a performer, too. The Earle Theatre at Missouri and Atlantic avenues has been replaced by a gas station, but in the twenties and thirties, vaudeville acts performed there. Skinny entered amateur shows and demonstrated his natural tap-dancing ability. He may have yearned to be a star, but his talents and future would lie in promoting other stars and running the day-to-day business of the Naughty Queen's favorite nightclub.

Nucky preserved his power, in part, by allowing others to have their own. His tolerance required cooperation, though: No one was to challenge his ultimate authority or show him disrespect. Skinny was smart enough to keep his ambition in check, and to treat Nucky as an elder statesmen, and there were no problems between the two men. But it was a different story with the fickle Naughty Queen, for she was beginning to look Skinny's way more often than Nucky's.

In the mid-thirties, a young trolley conductor from Philadelphia also sought his fortune in the "promised land" by the sea. Phil Barr was about thirty years old when he borrowed from friends and scraped together enough money to buy two houses on South Missouri Avenue, not far from where Skinny was born. He razed them and opened the 500 Café, an intimate nightclub and horse joint. Barr was a quiet, unassuming man, well-built with blonde hair, and he was said to be a Bob Hope look-alike.

During the day, chairs were centered in the club, and draperies were drawn, revealing horse-race results on blackboards. In the evenings, attractive girls graced the small stage, dancing the Charleston, the black bottom and the romantic Argentine tango with suave young men who imagined they were George Raft.

Barr understood the rules of Atlantic City, and he did not infringe upon the turf of the Queen's well-established subjects. Naturally, first and foremost, he respected Nucky. Barr's unobtrusive manner, amiability and courtesy gave him the necessary security to operate his business unmolested.

His wife had died, and he entrusted the rearing of his daughter, Catherine, to his manager, Harry Blackman, and his wife, Betty. He purchased a home in Ventnor, just below Atlantic City, and above the perils that the Naughty Queen offered. Ventnor's purity was no accident: Politicians actually had decided that illegal activities were to be limited to Atlantic City, and the so-called "downbeach" towns of Ventnor, Margate and Longport were to be off-limits.

Barr, for one, succumbed to the temptations that abounded in the Queen's domain. He had a love affair with Louise Mack, the owner of the Entertainers Club who infamously swept her customers' money off the bar and into the ice bucket.

Not everyone liked the Queen's naughtiness, however. One advocate for change was attorney Thomas D. Taggart Jr., a zealot who greatly worried Nucky and his crowd. Taggart was considered to be a "loud mouth," shrewd and possessed of raw guts. He was of medium height and build, and, like Nucky, had black hair and dark eyes. He was not handsome like Nucky, and he never married, living instead with his sisters in a rambling house behind the city's old library on Illinois Avenue.

Taggart also was a politician. From 1934 to 1937, he served in the state Assembly. He was elected to the state Senate in 1937 and served there until 1940. That same year, he became an Atlantic City commissioner. Taggart was a no-holds-barred type of official who kept dossiers and mug shots of prominent resort leaders. He often bragged, somewhat oddly: "I fear no mother's son in shoes or barefooted."

Nucky summoned Taggart to his cottage. At that point, Taggart did seem to fear one mother's son a bit as he and Nucky faced off. Nucky appeared angry, making Taggart nervous, but then he smiled and asked Taggart questions that his guest did not like. In turn, Nucky managed not to answer Taggart's questions. Taggart assured Nucky of his loyalty and dedication to the Republican Party.

"A drink?" Nucky asked.

Taggart declined, grabbing Nucky's hand, and pumping it until Nucky finally pulled it away.

"Boss," Taggart reconsidered, "I think I'll have a brandy."

Nucky laughed, his black eyes twinkling as he watched Taggart savor the "liquid gold."

"I heard about those records of yours," Nucky primed. "Lot of dynamite. If you need any help ... sing out."

"Now, Nucky, I didn't mean anything about you —" Taggart protested.

From then on, Taggart kept a dossier on Nucky. It probably contained some pretty juicy stuff, and it was about to get better.

On May 19, 1939, Nucky was arrested in Newark, New Jersey, and charged with income-tax evasion, according to records at the United States Penitentiary in Lewisburg, Pennsylvania.

Nucky's secretary, Maie Paxson, called him at home.

"Boss, the federal grand jury has just indicted you."

"What for?"

"Evasion of income taxes in the sum of $125,000 from the numbers business from 1936 to 1937."

"To hell with it!"

He was worried about the charge, and worried that he may have underestimated Taggart. He started paying particular attention to the senator's activities. Taggart was ambitious, and he spoke before church groups, preaching "hellfire and brimstone" about the gambling joints and the harlots who had turned Atlantic City into a modern Sodom. In May 1940, Taggart was elected a commissioner of Atlantic City, and his fellow commissioners appointed him mayor.

The commission election gave Taggart three public positions: judge of the Common Pleas Court, senator and now mayor. He gave up his judgeship and Senate seat and devoted himself to being mayor.

With Taggart as mayor, it appeared as if illegal gambling and prostitution were drifting out to sea. However, the dice rolled furtively, horse and numbers bets continued and winners were paid. Card and crap games went on as usual, and prostitution flourished.

Soon Taggart earned himself a reputation, and a *nom de guerre*: "Two-Gun Taggart." He may have been a prude, but this still was Atlantic City, where flamboyance in all things was required. As such, Taggart took to wearing a set of pearl-handled guns tucked Western-style into his belt as he raided the city's bawdy joints and houses of prostitution. His spies became legion, and he took special pleasure in recruiting Herman G. "Stumpy" Orman for his lineup.

Stumpy Orman, whose nickname referred to the withered little finger on his right hand, was a local businessman who got his start as a bootlegger and numbers racketeer. Time and legal business deals bought him a measure of respectability in his later years, and he was known locally for his ownership of the famous Million Dollar Pier. He was a tough man, but islanders have said that, all in all, he was a fair businessman.

Taggart's allegations that Orman's deals may not all have been aboveboard bothered Orman, who retaliated derogatorily by calling Taggart a "queer." That infuriated Taggart, and he ordered a special squad of police to entrap Orman.

Orman finally appealed to his friend, Frank S. "Hap" Farley, an attorney who one day himself would be boss of Atlantic City — though he would shudder at actually being called "boss." Farley called upon Nucky, but Nucky wanted no part of his and Orman's Taggart problem. He, after all, had his own Taggart problem with which to contend.

"You fellows will have to handle Taggart as best as you can," Nucky told Farley flatly.

Now it was getting serious, with Taggart spreading enough fear to rile people like Nucky and Orman and to shift the power balance to himself. The tremulous question was raised: Did Taggart now have enough power to change the Naughty Queen's way of life?

Taggart bragged to newspapers and radio stations: "I'm against the riffraff, and I intend to eliminate horse joints and gambling. They will no longer reap a golden harvest."

Many islanders lost sleep over promises like those. No more horse parlors? No more gambling dens? How would they survive? Taggart's weapons and rhetoric unnerved them, especially when he called the city the "badlands."

And he was relentless, declaring: "Atlantic City is a closed town, closed to the bums, crooks and pickpockets. The city will no longer be a happy hunting ground for them."

Taggart now bore the brunt of the Queen's subjects' displeasure. They no longer could depend upon the illegal activities that infused the local economy with jobs, payoffs and bribes because they were afraid of his zealousness, suspicions, raids and arrests.

Taggart cruised the city, searching for racketeers and gamblers. On one such outing, a bullet hit his windshield. He escaped injury, but his fury was volcanic. He placed an ad in the *Atlantic City Press*, proclaiming:

> You are being asked to act as a tool for racketeers and the underworld characters who have, heretofore, lined their pockets with "gold" at the expense of you and your families. You are being asked to turn control of city affairs to the rule of illegitimate groups and "gravy boys" who have fattened their purses and emptied yours by driving visitors away from Atlantic City.

Islanders gossiped about the advertisement, but they went furtively on their way, with business as usual. They were not offended by their society. The Queen's subjects respected the joint owners who had shown kindness and generosity to society's less fortunate members.

One such example was "Six-foot Lizzie," a bulk of a woman with a hunched back. Curvature of the spine had reduced Lizzie's height to something in the vicinity of four feet. She had brassy red hair that seemed more butchered than cut, and she wore a toothless smile, behind which she smacked tobacco against her gums. She carried her worldly possessions in a wagon, but when it broke down, she used an orange crate. Her job was to clean latrines for the guys who owned the joints. Lizzie slept in empty buildings during the summer, but the joint owners rented a room for her in the winter. She became a landmark and was photographed with tourists and islanders alike. When she died, Phil Barr buried her, and the other joint owners paid their respects.

The Hearst newspapers had been relentless in their efforts to destroy Nucky Johnson, and Hearst prodded federal authorities to clean up the island. In 1937, rumors spread throughout the city that J. Edgar Hoover, head of the Federal Bureau of Investigation, and Walter Winchell, the famous columnist, had entered the city in disguise and visited a casino in one of the clubs.

America listened to Winchell every Sunday night on the radio, and his signature opening to "Mr. and Mrs. America and all the ships at sea" was well-known.

Hoover soon established headquarters at the Traymore Hotel. The raids intensified. G-men, state troopers and local police assumed their roles. They were supposed to be the good guys, but islanders were suffering. Every joint, casino and nightclub suffered losses as equipment was smashed, and staff were arrested, fined and jailed.

The raids were devastating islanders, who worried about putting food on their tables, clothing on their children and paying their rent. It may have appeared that peace had broken out between the authorities and the racketeers, but the truth was the racketeers merely submerged their activities, holding games in private homes and hideouts. To make a living, it became necessary for some dealers to don tuxedos and travel daily to northern New Jersey, where gambling was held on estates.

Men who took the rap and did time for Nucky were given jobs, set up in business, or otherwise rewarded financially upon their release. Islanders needed their boss nearby — no one else could even begin to control the island's competing factions.

Despite the ongoing raids and continued covert gaming, people knew the city's illegal activities continued. Outsiders considered the Queen incorrigible. She smiled because her coffers filled up again with lovely dollars, and she had found men, once more, to take care of her — some state troopers were taking bribes to tip off joint owners about impending raids.

Skinny D'Amato had become a casino manager for his friend and boyhood pal Jack "Colby" Berenato at Luigi's Bar and Restaurant, located at Arkansas (which was, and still is, pronounced as AR-Kansas rather than Ar-kansaw) and Pacific avenues. Probably no one knew more about gambling than Skinny, who loved it with a passion and made plenty of money from his betting acumen.

Berenato had a husky build, a receding hairline and a quiet manner. He was a cautious man with a tough exterior. He owned two Buicks.

One was for transportation; the other was parked for security in front of his restaurant — just in case anyone had thoughts of robbing him.

In addition to Barr and Colby Berenato, Sam and Frank Camarota owned the Hialeah Club at Michigan and Atlantic avenues. They had legal entertainment on the ground floor, and a casino above the club, where one could bet on horses and numbers as well.

Barr had set up a casino in the back of the Garibaldi Club, a hotel next door to his 500 Café. Italian immigrants had founded the club and named it for the Italian patriot Giuseppe Garibaldi. The men played card games such as sette-mezza, or seven and a half; briscolo; scoppo; and pinochle. They also assisted fellow immigrants in their adjustment to American culture, gave free music lessons and purchased instruments for children.

On Stenton Avenue near the Boardwalk, one could find The Bath and Turf Club, an elegant house in which customers dined on Chinese food. The club had an intriguing secret, however: Those who chose to gamble would stand in front of a mural in the foyer, push a button, and cross a "bridge" to a house on the next street. Nucky, naturally, had an interest in the club, as did manager Charlie Schwartz and the famed gangster Meyer Lansky. Business flourished in the lovely guesthouse and its covert casino, and Lansky himself frequented the club. He demanded complete anonymity, which he was granted with the utmost respect.

Barr and other joint owners paid a fin, or five dollars, a head to "luggers," and wealthy bettors were whisked from the train station at Missouri and Atlantic avenues to the waiting casinos.

Barr's reputation as a decent guy was undisputed, and he endeared himself to islanders with acts of compassion. When distraught women came to him because their husbands had gambled their paychecks, they were refunded the entire amount. The next time their husbands tried to gamble, they received a stern warning: "If you can't afford to gamble, stay out of my joint!"

Most joint owners followed suit. It was an unwritten code of honor. Besides, they didn't want any trouble, such as adverse publicity, or worse, police intervention.

In today's casinos, surveillance is a hi-tech affair that can be conducted both on the gaming floor itself and from rooms hidden above the gambling areas. Pit bosses watch the action on the floor, while the state Division of Gaming Enforcement and Casino Control Commission both have people stationed in every casino property and have placed cameras strategically to cover virtually every inch of the gaming floor — they can just about see the dirt under dealers' fingernails.

A patron in a casino today can be followed by four cameras and never know it, according to the Casino Control Commission. Perhaps most intriguing of all the surveillance devices are the observation stations that lie above the casino floor and are separated from it by one-way glass. These stations no longer are required in new casino construction, but when gambling was legalized in Atlantic City, the state wasn't taking any chances with the deceptive Queen.

Back in Barr's day, the Queen's devious qualities were considered an asset. And the no-tech surveillance system consisted of guards standing on ladders, scanning dealers and players alike for cheating and other funny business. On one occasion, a dealer had a C-note sticking out of his silk shirt. A guard signaled Barr, who confronted the thief.

"What the hell are you doing? Robbing me?" Barr asked.

"G-geez, Phil, it flew into my pocket."

"That's a lot of crap. Don't you ever do that again. If I can't trust my dealers, out they go."

"I swear I won't do it again."

Another time, during Passover, a dealer requested fried matzo and eggs. The chef sent the waiter to neighborhood stores, all of which had sold out of matzo. The chef apologized to the dealer and offered to make him something else, but the dealer was adamant. His Jewish faith would not allow him to eat bread or other leavened foods during Passover.

"I want matzo and eggs!" he declared.

The chef was in a quandary. He could not get matzo, yet he needed to make the dealer a proper meal. In his desperation and frustration, a humorous — to him — solution presented itself. The chef grabbed a straw hat, chopped it up into bits and cooked it with the eggs. He winked at the waiter who served the dealer.

The dealer thanked the chef and took a bite. He immediately spat it out, pounded the table and screamed at the chef while everyone roared with laughter. The dealer didn't think the chef should get a second chance with his joke, so he made sure the next day to bring his own matzo. Then he watched the chef cook it with eggs.

Players never left a casino empty-handed. Depending on their level of play — how much they lost — they were given something called a *vigorege*. Not to be confused with "vigorish" (also known as the "juice" and "chop"), which was the commission charged on a bet, *vigorege* today is called "comps" for the complimentary services that are accorded some high-roller gamblers. In the casinos of Barr's era, *vigorege* could be a "bean," or one dollar; a "fin," five dollars; or a "sawbuck," ten dollars. If players came from out of town, they received a C-note for a room, a meal and train fare back home.

Gamblers followed a convenient protocol in which women played games of chance during the day, and their husbands, some with their girlfriends, played at night. This avoided many sorts of embarrassments. Some elegant, wealthy women who went "slumming" had a fascination for the dealers who were part of the bawdy underworld — and so removed from their upscale day-to-day experiences. Many brief but torrid romances took place between members of the two vastly different worlds. An equality prevailed long enough to satisfy primal needs, and afterward, the dealers were nicely compensated with generous tips.

Not all outings ended with satisfied customers, however. One evening, club owners Babette and Dan Stebbins were decked out for a night on the town. They were considered high society on the island, and as such, they were obligated to be seen and "give a play" to other nightclubs.

As they stepped out of their car, a bullet struck Dan in his belt buckle, and bounced off. It scared the heck out of him and Babette. Dan concluded that Lady Luck was on his side that night, and even though that was the only recorded assassination attempt on him, it was quite enough. He became and remained an extremely cautious man afterward.

The government, the do-gooder one, was playing it safe, too. Secret Service agents dressed themselves as "wise guys" and mingled with the crowd at the Paddock International, a club located at Illinois and Atlantic avenues. Zorita and her eight-foot "Arabian blue snake" were featured there, as was Lenny Ross, a risque comedian. The Secret Service men, concerned with Ross's obscenities, watched who came and went at the club. It seemed no one was immune from the eyes and ears of the federal government.

Islanders have related story upon story about Nucky's kindness, compassion and generosity. One of the most touching is that of Joseph D'Amico, the kind-hearted tailor who helped Atlantic City's prostitutes, and his daughter Carrie, who was seriously ill with tuberculosis. Carrie's doctor had advised her father to place the girl in Pine Rest, a hospital for tuberculous patients on the mainland in Northfield, New Jersey.

D'Amico was disillusioned, however, when hospital officials could not accommodate Carrie. He called the doctor.

"Joe," the doctor said, "Call Nucky. He'll get her in."

"I don't know him personally."

"Doesn't matter with him."

D'Amico made the call, and Nucky promised to get back to him within a week. True to his word, Nucky called D'Amico back and told him to get Carrie ready.

Later, a limousine pulled up in front of D'Amico's store, which still is in existence, and Louie Kessel went inside to help Carrie's father with her luggage. Islanders gathered around the limousine, but Nucky did not want the attention. He told Kessel to drive D'Amico and Carrie to Pine Rest, where Carrie died shortly thereafter.

But Nucky's days as boss were numbered, as age, the government and the Queen's younger suitors began to close in on him. He discovered that the FBI had wiretapped his phone, an illegal tactic, and from that day on, he did not use his telephone for business calls.

But the federal government was not about to give up. One summer evening, Nucky went to Asbury Park with a friend. He left Louie behind to keep an eye on the house. Louie was as loyal as they come, but he wasn't the smartest guy, and he wasn't nearly suspicious enough. The day after Nucky had gone, Louie sat outside of Nucky's home, stripped to the waist to keep cool against the heat and humming the "Dance of the Cossacks," his favorite music.

A man walked by and called out to him: "Mr. Kessel, is the boss home? He knows me. I'm the owner ... "

"Say, friend, I don't know you."

"I came to Nucky's party with Joe Moss."

"Oh yeah, gotcha. What can I do for you?"

"The town's crowded, and I can't get a room."

"Well, the boss ain't here. You can stay in the cottage."

"Great," the undercover agent replied.

The agent had a night of rejoicing, scavenging through Nucky's closets and files. He could not believe his luck. In the morning, he left with enough evidence to bring Nucky to trial. It had been so easy.

The government also got Nucky on what might be called tax evasion through "money laundering" — or maybe the case of the pillowcases. Agents dressed themselves as derelicts, loitered outside Nucky's cathouses and took note of the laundry deliveries. The agents then multiplied those amounts to figure Nucky's yearly income from his *bagnios* — and from that determined what he owed in unpaid taxes.

After a pretrial hearing, Jersey City's Frank "I Am The Law" Hague visited Nucky and extended his hand in friendship. Even though the two men had not been friends previously, Hague knew that they both loved their respective cities and worked in their very different ways to benefit them.

"Frank, I've never hurt anyone intentionally," Nucky said. "I'll be pleased and happy to answer to the good Lord. The ingratitude of islanders and kings is well-known to me."

Hague nodded in knowing agreement.

The Queen's subjects were abuzz on street corners and in restaurants, bars and joints. Those who were jealous of Nucky and his power enjoyed his predicament. His enemies hovered over newspapers like vultures who could read. The majority of islanders, however, many of them the hard-working people, uttered "Our Fathers" in church on Sundays for their boss and benefactor.

Nucky was released on bail to await trial. Then he vanished, and even Louie didn't know where he was. Louie was worried, perhaps doubly so because it was his own mistake that had aided Nucky's arrest. But as suddenly as Nucky had disappeared, he reappeared. Louie found Nucky in his own bedroom, where he leaned against a pole, smoking a cigarette.

"Hey, Boss, don't do dat again," a shaken Louie implored. "I've been worried about you."

"Draw my bath, not too hot or too cold," Nucky said as he brushed off Louie's concern. "Tell Mame to cook me a dozen eggs."

"Where were you?" Louie asked, continuing the conversation he wanted to have.

"My wife ... Mabel died in Denver, and I needed quiet time," Nucky said. He walked toward the window, listened to the crash of the pounding, foaming waves. Whatever else was on his mind, he was glad to be home.

On August 29, 1939, Nucky was found guilty of tax evasion and sentenced to ten years in federal prison. It would be his time away from the Naughty Queen, and not the fact that he had a criminal conviction, that would prove his ultimate undoing.

"Boss, how much time are we serving?" Louie asked.

"We?" Nucky answered. "Are we pregnant or something? You're not going."

"If you go, I go."

"Louie," Nucky replied. He was shaking his head, but he genuinely was touched by Louie's devotion.

Prior to his sentencing, Nucky had met with a government lawyer. The men shook hands.

"Mr. Johnson, have a seat."

"No, thanks."

"Mr. Johnson, the United States government is inclined to deal with you leniently. After all, you're fifty-eight years old."

"I'm glad to hear that."

"We want certain information from you, and you will only serve a year and a day."

"That's a long sentence for a man who hasn't done anything wrong."

"Are you saying you won't cooperate?"

"I'm saying I won't be an informer," Nucky answered. "I consider your proposal an insult. Good day."

Before Nucky departed for prison, his close friends gathered at a cocktail lounge for a sendoff of sorts. The group included Harold Hoffman, Johnny D'Agostino, Warren Barbour, Louie Kessel, John Murtland, Herman Taylor and Flossie Osbeck. Nucky squeezed Flossie's hand and proposed a toast.

"Gentlemen," he announced, "Flossie and I are getting married in the Presbyterian Church on Pennsylvania and Pacific avenues. A toast to my future bride ..."

Flossie laughed with a tinkling melody that Nucky would remember for the rest of his days.

"The big lug is marrying me so he'll have someone to visit him in jail," she joked.

"That's right," Nucky chuckled.

The couple were married on July 31, 1941, the night before Nucky's sentencing, in the Presbyterian Church. It was a desperately romantic act, what Flossie had wanted for so long, but not at all the way she had envisioned it.

Nucky went to prison on August 11th of that year, leaving the couple little opportunity to honeymoon or build their marriage. That would have to come later, and it did. But for now, the circumstances of their marriage sealed rather than began their lives together.

Before Nucky left Atlantic City for prison, he had spoken with state Senator Frank S. "Hap" Farley, who was considered by many to be Nucky's protege.

"I'm turning the whole thing over to you," Nucky told him. "Take good care of things."

"Nuck, it'll be just like you left it," Farley promised.

"See that Flossie gets my paycheck from the county treasurer's office."

"Sure, Nuck."

Louie drove Nucky to prison in a limousine, accompanied by Flossie, Johnny D'Agostino and Johnny's brother Carmen. Nucky seemed more a visiting dignitary than an inmate-in-waiting as his limo wound through the Pennsylvania mountains to reach Lewisburg Penitentiary in the Susquehanna Valley.

The weight of Nucky's imminent confinement increased with every mountain turn. A sudden, desperate longing for the Naughty Queen overcame him. As he drove away from his life, he remembered the stars in the clear nighttime skies, and he recalled his first bride. She had been so lovely, and so young. But she was gone from Atlantic City, and now he was gone as well. He grabbed Flossie's hand, kissed it and held it close to him, weeping. Flossie kissed his cheek, her tears mixed with his, and silence hung in the air as they rode.

When they stepped out of their cars, Nucky, Flossie and their friends glanced at each other with sadness and anxiety. Flossie bawled.

"Stop it, girl," Nucky urged. "Dry up your tears. I'm sorry I can't take you on a honeymoon."

"You big lug ..." Flossie sobbed.

"Louie, take care of her," Nucky said.

"Sure, Boss," Louie replied, holding back his own tears.

Nucky's retreat into the prison was so much more an ending than a beginning. He may have suspected it — if so, he kept quiet about it. But his days as boss were over. The cell doors hadn't even clanged shut on him before the Naughty Queen took up with another man. Hap Farley would be running the place now.

Nucky's lifelong optimism failed him now in prison. The son of a jailer was now locked up himself, and confinement was depressing. Nucky always had been in control, but now the government was telling him when to rise, when to eat and when to go to bed. It was monotonous, and stifling.

An officer softened the initial blow, greeting him with the words, "Mr. Johnson, you have a lot of friends here. The word has spread about your arrival."

"Thanks," Nucky replied, grateful for the jailhouse hospitality.

The stars from the small window of his cell appeared so distant and so pale, and Nucky missed the sound of the pounding surf that lolled him to sleep every night. His deal-making opportunities were small-scale now, too, though he did make accommodations to his new circumstances. When another inmate offered to make Nucky's bed every day and get him fresh eggs for breakfast in exchange for two packs of cigarettes, Nucky accepted the offer.

In a bit of unintended irony, Nucky was assigned to the laundry room. There, some inmates recalled his kindnesses to their families. And those of color remembered that Nucky had been an equal-opportunity boss.

One inmate, "Preacher" Washington, called out to him as Nucky approached the bathroom.

"Mr. Johnson, don't go in there yet," Preacher suggested.

"Why not?" Nucky asked. "What's going on?"

"Violet and Sweetness is making love ... they is a disgrace to a disgrace," Preacher said.

Nucky chuckled. He was getting used to the homosexual lust that permeated the prison, but for his part, he would hold out for women in general, and one named Flossie in particular.

In the meantime, Nucky settled in to prison life as best he could.

At Sunday Mass, an inmate called "Mother McCarthy" played the organ sweetly, and Nucky still contemplated converting to Roman Catholicism. Mother McCarthy was an old prisoner who originally came from Greenwich Village in New York City, but prison had been his home for a long time.

On December 7, 1941, the Japanese bombed Pearl Harbor. Shock, anger and a patriotic fervor reverberated all the way to Nucky's Pennsylvania prison. Prisoners wanted to do or die for their country, but few ultimately were chosen.

The editor of the inmate newspaper, *The Lens*, got a bit carried away with his loyalties and claimed in an editorial that the Unknown Soldier was an ex-convict. The Associated Press picked up the story, leading several patriotic organizations to contact the warden with their complaints and outrage. The editor of *The Lens* was demoted all the way to the scullery.

Louie and Flossie visited Nucky weekly, and sometimes twice weekly, at what Nucky called "the college." Johnny often came along with them. After one of their trips to Lewisburg, Louie and Flossie were returning home after dropping Johnny off in Egg Harbor City when a car slammed broadside into their limousine. Flossie had a few scratches, but Louie had been on the side of the car that was hit. He was in bad shape. Rescuers had to pry him out of the car. When they put him on a stretcher, he smiled at Flossie. But his last thoughts were of Nucky.

"Tell the boss ..." he began to say. Louie died amid Flossie's sobs. When word of Louie's death reached Nucky, his grief and powerlessness left him despondent. He pleaded to attend Louie's funeral, but prison officials forbade him from going.

Nucky served four years of his ten-year sentence. On August 15, 1945, the day he was released from prison, Johnny and Carmen dropped Flossie off at a motel while they went to get her bridegroom.

When Nucky saw Johnny and Carmen, he was overwhelmed. As he embraced them, he confided, "I was raised in the Mays Landing jail, and for a time, I thought I'd die in jail."

"Nucky, you're sixty-two years old," Johnny said. "You can still enjoy life."

That night, Nucky and Flossie enjoyed their delayed honeymoon. In the morning, they went home to Atlantic City. Nucky was jubilant. He strolled the Boardwalk, inhaled the salty air and believed he really could enjoy life again.

He felt young.

The news of Nucky's release spread through the city, to mixed reactions. Islanders who recalled with fondness Nucky's kind gestures were glad to have him home. But those whom Nucky had left in charge of the Naughty Queen had been overcome by her and had taken the city over in return. They considered Nucky a has-been and saw no need to share with him.

To make matters worse, "Two-Gun" Taggart got state and local law enforcers to step up their campaigns and raids against the gambling and prostitution rackets that so many city residents depended upon to support themselves and their families.

The attention was most unwanted at Barr's 500 Café, which was surrounded by an Atlantic City police squad led by Chief Earl Butcher. The *Atlantic City Press* reported in a March 13, 1941, article that Barr, Morris Zatlin (who was a suspect and had been a fugitive in the Dan Stebbins belt-buckle shooting) and nine others were arrested in that raid, while some 80 customers were questioned. Among those nabbed was the infamous Cappy Hoffman. Police discovered various gambling devices and an elaborately equipped horse-race betting setup. In Barr's elegantly furnished apartment above the cafe, law enforcers found a safe containing five thousand dollars in cash, and a buzzer to warn his men of impending problems.

Barr and some of his dealers were jailed in the episode. While incarcerated, Barr suffered a heart attack. His lawyer obtained his release on medical grounds. Barr returned to his apartment, where a letter from the Internal Revenue Service brought him more distress:

You are hereby notified there is due, owing and unpaid from Philip J.

Barr to the United States of America, Bureau of Internal Revenue, the sum of $44,912.54, plus accrued interest at 6 percent per annum until the tax is paid in full. You are notified that all property, right to property, money credits, bank accounts, in your possession belonging to Philip J. Barr ... have been seized and levied for payment of such aforesaid tax.

Phil Barr had lost everything. A broken man, he suffered a second heart attack. This one proved fatal. His only child, Catherine, remained with Betty and Harry Blackman, who raised her as their own.

WhEN Nucky surveyed the damage his absence had done to his position in Atlantic City, he realized it was bad. He had been forced into retirement from public life by those whom he had entrusted with running the Naughty Queen. There was no job waiting for him, and worse, Flossie told Nucky she had not received the county treasurer's paycheck that Hap Farley was supposed to have sent.

For his part, it wouldn't do for the ambitious Farley to maintain an association with the tarnished Nucky. Still, Nucky was shocked, offended and upset that Flossie had not been taken care of when he was away.

Johnny hired Nucky and Flossie as sales representatives for Renault Winery. The couple moved to a rented home on Elberon Avenue and passed pleasant evenings on their spacious porch, where Nucky sometimes considered his past, and present, lives. His observations held more reflection than rancor, despite what he saw as betrayal by Farley and his crowd.

"When I left," he told Flossie at one point, "they were broke. In four years, they've become millionaires."

Gone were the days when Nucky would entertain swarms of people at fancy parties, leave big tips, stroll the boardwalk as if he owned it, fix people's problems, as well as his own, and show charity toward the disadvantaged.

In autumn of the following year, a testimonial dinner was held for Senator Farley, and the new establishment "forgot" to invite Nucky and Flossie. It was an oversight that Nucky could not ignore.

At the dinner, which was attended by some six hundred rank-and-file Republicans, Nucky entered through a back door and stepped onto the stage, where he congratulated Farley. The embarrassed senator wore a frozen smile as whispers spread throughout the room:

"My God, it's Nucky Johnson," the surprised guests said. "Boys, the Boss is back."

Nucky's revenge was for him a cherished moment. But Nucky was a ghost from the past, and like him, the moment would soon be no more than a memory for most of those attending the dinner.

Among the people who did remember Nucky were the city's black leaders. An important election was pending, and they sought his counsel by calling upon him at his home.

"Boss, what do you think of this slate?" one man asked.

"Haven't made up my mind yet," Nucky dodged. He didn't care for what the new bosses of the city had done to him, but he did not want to alienate them either. He also did not want to offend the black community, which he had supported in his day, and which had supported him in return.

Meanwhile, rumors ran through the local Republican hierarchy that voter sentiment was not entirely with the GOP. The party was worried. Two days before the election, the new bosses sought the old one's endorsement. It was payback time for Nucky, but he did it with the class and style they so singularly lacked.

"I've made no compromises in my life," Nucky told them. "I've never betrayed a friend and never kicked a man when he's down."

It gave Nucky some satisfaction to instill a modicum of guilt in those men, and to send them off empty-handed. After they left, Nucky strolled the Boardwalk, tipping his hat to women and nodding to men who acknowledged him. He thought, "If sin has touched the island, it has also held life, laughter and gaiety."

Nucky reflected, too, on his heyday: the beautiful women he had known, influential friends, great names in show business and the hustle, bustle and glamour of it all.

"I'll never see times like that again," he thought, "a pity, and a shame."

He was asked frequently if he would seek office again. His pithy response did not vary:

"I've got all I can handle in running ahead of the undertaker," he would say.

Nucky's new job kept him busy. His and Flossie's work for the winery involved travel around southern New Jersey. While they were away on one business excursion, word reached them that Johnny had been killed in an automobile accident. Nucky was distraught at the loss of his best friend. After Johnny's funeral, Nucky joined a party of laymen on a retreat to a monastery, where he sought solace among those who led reflective lives.

A nother boss was about to fade from the scene as well. As mayor, Thomas "Two-Gun" Taggart had practically declared war to clean up Atlantic City. He rattled it, and its residents, with constant raids and the consequent adverse publicity and loss of revenue those bombardments brought. On the evening of Sept. 4, 1950, Taggart strolled the city's streets. He entered a store on Pacific Avenue and made a phone call.

His death began as he hung up the telephone. Suddenly in distress, Taggart leaned against a pinball machine. A clerk ran to his aid.

"Boss, can I help you?"

"It's nothing," Taggart replied. "I'll be all right."

"Boss, I used to have those attacks, until I found this tonic."

"What is it?"

Taggart listened to the clerk's instructions and went home with some of the tonic. He ate sparingly and retired to his bedroom, where he poured some tonic in a glass and sniffed it. There was no discernible odor, so he drank the contents. In the dim light, he unlaced his shoes, leaned back on his bed and groped for the pillow. But he was beyond the ability of the tonic to help him.

By morning, on September 5, 1950, the "Wyatt Earp" of the island was dead of a heart attack. Taggart was 47 years old.

The *Atlantic City Press*, which had championed Taggart's career and integrity, did not fail him in death and even went so far as to label him a "martyr to the cause of better government."

"Well done, good and faithful servant," the newspaper eulogized.

But not everyone felt so kindly toward Taggart. The mayor had been the subject of a recall movement during his first year in office. Atlantic City's commissioners bypassed that recall effort by approving two resolutions (while Taggart was out of town) that stripped him of his authority over various city agencies — including the police department, which he had driven to distraction with excessive orders.

Local scuttlebutt holds that the recall drive began after Taggart zealously began arresting the elderly men and women who played bingo on the Boardwalk. According to oldtimers, islanders were outraged to see their parents and grandparents carted off in paddy wagons like common criminals. (Several thousand signatures, not enough to force the mayor's ouster, were gathered.) Angry, and feeling betrayed, Taggart damaged his career further by distancing himself from the Farley political machine.

Farley had learned from the masters, including Nucky, and would put into place a political-patronage system so effective that it would continue operating after his death. He was six feet tall, husky, and wore his hair slicked back and parted in the middle behind his receding hairline. The eight-term state senator from Atlantic County also wore a perpetual plastic smile; he knew when to grant favors, and to whom.

Farley was a powerhouse of a man whose vision and tenacity created the Atlantic City Expressway. The east-west superhighway brings millions of people a year from the Philadelphia area to the Jersey Shore region, and, of course, Atlantic City. In recognition of Farley, the expressway's administrative plaza was named for him in 1977. He also laid the groundwork for The Richard Stockton College of New Jersey and Atlantic Community College, which has become known for its fine culinary program.

In Farley's day, a person in political life would have to go pretty far, certainly to another county and possibly to another state, to get away from his political machine. Farley ruled his county and Atlantic City for 31 years, from 1940 to 1971 and controlled the resort's political movements to the smallest twitch. His regime was an institution that in 1951 would fascinate and appall even the pros — Washington, D.C., politicians.

Frank Sherman Farley was born in Atlantic City on December 1, 1901, the youngest of ten children. Nicknamed "Hap" for his happy-go-lucky personality, Farley attended Wenonah Military Academy and the University of Pennsylvania. He earned his law degree from prestigious Georgetown University in 1925.

He returned to run Atlantic City from his perch as a state senator. In the Statehouse in Trenton, Farley pushed for legislation favorable to his home turf. He got around a state law prohibiting such pork-barrel politics by introducing bills bearing the phrase "for Fifth Class counties bordering on the ocean" and other stipulations that would cause the legislation to apply (sometimes solely) to Atlantic County. He also avoided the appearance of conflicts of interest by having other senators sponsor some of his Atlantic County bills and returned the favor by sponsoring theirs.

Despite Atlantic City and Atlantic County being bastions of Republican Party control, Farley persuaded President Lyndon B. Johnson to bring the 1964 Democratic National Convention to Atlantic City.

Farley also was a delegate to the Republican National Convention from 1944 to 1968. In 1968, he made a move to back Richard M. Nixon for president. That move split the New Jersey delegation and dashed the presidential candidacy of Nelson Rockefeller, who would have to settle for the vice president's job after Nixon's fall from grace and replacement by Gerald Ford.

Shocked and furious, some politicians never forgave Farley. But the gambit paid off for him: It put Nixon on the ballot as the Republican Party's candidate. When Nixon won the presidency, Farley had a pal in a high place. Nixon never forgot to ask, fondly, about his friend Hap whenever he met representatives from New Jersey.

Farley forged a reputation for himself as he forged a newer reputation for Atlantic City. He was discreet, as the times required, and he replaced Atlantic City's sin-city aura with laws aimed at bettering the city and increasing tourism. Of course, Atlantic City still had its houses of prostitution and gambling once Taggart lost power, but they operated a bit more carefully than they had in Nucky's day.

Ironically, it was Taggart who initially endorsed Farley. On June 2, 1941, Mayor Taggart spoke to the Atlantic County Republican Commission about Atlantic City under his auspices and promoted Farley to the party's county-chairman job following the resignation of Bertram Whitman.

"We can get along without the riff-raff and no longer will those in illegal business consider themselves running the community," the *Atlantic City Press* quoted Taggart as saying.

A rally cheer went up from the audience as Taggart backed Farley to head the commission. That day he would not have believed that he and Farley soon would become bitter enemies. Taggart finished his speech by singling out Farley.

"I am ready for a real Republican party," he said, "and there's the boy who's going to give it to you."

The details of the Taggart-Farley falling out are vague, but Taggart and his raids clearly were alienating voters, and perhaps not coincidentally, Farley did not deal with crime and the city's vast illegal enterprises with the same fervor as the mayor.

As Taggart fought to hold onto his mayoral post, Farley was enjoying increased acceptance and respect. In June 1943, the two would attend a public-utilities hearing over an attempt by the Pennsylvania-Reading Seashore Lines to end summer weekend service from Philadelphia to Atlantic City. Neither man would raise his eyes to the other's gaze as both argued to keep the weekend rail service running.

Farley was as discreet as Nucky was flamboyant. Steve Neal, a staff writer for *The Philadelphia Inquirer*, reported in Farley's 1977 obituary a conversation in which Herbert J. Stern, the U.S. attorney who had prosecuted members of the senator's machine, was asked why Farley himself was never convicted of a crime.

"We never developed any evidence that implicated Frank Farley ... It may just indicate that he was in it for power and not for money," Stern said.

That's not to say that Farley was opposed to money, however. He and his wife, Marie "Honey," lived in a modest home in Ventnor, but as the attorney for the Atlantic City Race Course, Farley legally held one million dollars worth of its stock.

In addition to their differences in character, Farley saw what the excesses of his mentor had wrought. Atlantic City's booming rackets were audacious, and so appalled the Treasury and Justice departments that decades after agents wrote their report on Nucky, shock still reverberates from their words:

> Further, the methods of operation of these rackets were absolutely wide open. They made no attempt whatever to conceal their activities — the horse rooms were located on the principal business avenue of Atlantic City and their doors were open to whoever wanted to walk in; the houses of prostitution were segregated mainly in one ward of the city, but they made no pretense of hiding the nature of their business; the "numbers" game was played everywhere as though it were not in violation of the New Jersey gambling statutes. It was difficult to find a store in which "numbers" were not written.

Noting the city's small size, 66,000 people living in a space eight miles long by a half mile wide, the report continued:

> ... it is obvious that the police department could not help being cognizant of these violations of law. As a matter of fact, the investigation by the Treasury Agents disclosed that all the law enforcement agencies of Atlantic City and Atlantic County not only were well aware of these conditions but actively regulated, protected and at times even assisted these rackets.

The report then listed the fee schedule that the police charged for protection: Horse rooms, $160 per week; numbers banks, $100 per week; and brothels, $50 per week in winter and $100 per week in summer.

It didn't take a political genius like Farley to see that such indiscretion was not expedient. During his 31 years in power, Farley shunned appearances of shadiness, and he even disliked being called "boss."

Very publicly, Farley pushed in the Senate for issues that played well back home: legalized gambling, more industry and better roads and education. Farley also attended all but two Senate sessions, missed due to illness, in his long career.

As the city's vice industry went underground, Farley worked on his vision for the resort. He brought the Garden State Parkway, the main north-south highway, to the Shore and southern New Jersey. His work resulted in the creation of the Atlantic City Race Course and the Atlantic City State Marina, which was renamed the Frank S. Farley Marina in 1971.

Farley created Atlantic City's Luxury Tax, which gave the resort the money to rebuild beaches after storms and make various city improvements to attract more tourism. Early on, he established the Fishing Conservation Commission in 1946 to protect coastal jetties.

Throughout his career, which began with a stint in the state Assembly and continued with his Senate position and, interestingly, Nucky's old job as Atlantic County treasurer, Farley and his wife attended dinner parties, galas and testimonials for him and other politicians. His Republican loyalty may have led to his particular taste in collectibles — elephant figurines. Those with their trunks turned up symbolized luck, and they were the only ones Farley would collect.

Like Nucky, Farley's inclusionary policies helped blacks gain government positions, but these jobs often benefited Farley more than the city's disadvantaged population on the North Side. According to an August 1971 article in *Philadelphia Magazine* by writer Greg Walter, Farley gave public positions to blacks, but he then ignored the decrepit conditions in their home bases. Urban-renewal funds that could have gone to black neighborhoods instead went to higher-income white areas where Farley's friends lived.

Farley died at home in his sleep of heart failure on Saturday, September 24, 1977, at the age of seventy-five. Thousands of people from all walks of life attended his viewing and funeral Mass at St. Nicholas of Tolentine Roman Catholic Church on Pacific Avenue. The Reverend George Riley, vice president of Villanova University and a friend of Farley's, eulogized him as: "a man who liked to be liked and had to court dislike through the scars of leadership." He also said Farley kept intact his Christian faith and his desire to help others.

"We shall miss him, but he will go on living in the monuments he has made and in the memories he has left," Riley said.

Farley's death was accompanied by a great many articles in newspapers commemorating his work. But there also were newspaper editorials that tempered Farley's acclaim by criticizing his not-so-saintly reputation for quiet involvement in the rackets.

Islanders considered Farley compassionate and generous. Those who had sick, crippled or mentally challenged children who could not be cared for at home could depend upon Farley's personal intervention in finding them the proper institution. His often-stated philosophy was to do things right, help, be nice to people, pass good legislation, be honest and don't run away from problems.

He lost a bid for re-election in 1971 to Dr. Joseph McGahn, a Democrat. When Farley died in 1977, Frank J. Prendergast, the longtime political editor of *The* (Atlantic City) *Press*, retold a story of that loss. It seemed that everyone who the former senator encountered would tell him, "I voted for you." Fed up by what Farley saw as their lack of sincerity, he finally commented, "If they all voted for me, how did I lose?"

Atlantic City being what it was, there always was speculation on how many layers a story had between the public version and the truth. In Farley's case, many believed he was not really the one in charge. That honor went to none other than Orman, the bootlegger and racketeer turned "legitimate" businessman.

There were rumors that Orman, a short, slightly built man with dark hair, bullied the tall, broad-shouldered Farley, and that in one fit of pique, he actually punched the senator in the face!

Belligerence aside, many a damsel considered Orman good-looking, or at least rich enough that his looks and mangled finger perhaps were secondary concerns. As a young man, Stumpy had married and divorced. He preferred the single life and died that way in 1995 in Florida, where he had retired many years before. He was eighty-seven years old.

Stumpy was admired for his business acumen and fairness in negotiating deals. He was not one to take chances, however, and slept soundly knowing that Babe Marcella, his bodyguard, was sitting just outside his bedroom door with his gun cocked. Marcella, a man made of solid, rippling muscle, also served as Stumpy's chauffeur and confidante.

Part II: Skinny

W hen the Japanese bombed Pearl Harbor and America entered World War II, the Naughty Queen solemnly, and judiciously, put her jewels away. Her neon lights were snuffed, and her subjects were told to place dark screens or shades on store windows, especially on those facing the sea to the east. Particular attention was accorded the Boardwalk's oceanfront stores, restaurants, bars and hotels.

The Sherwin-Williams paint company had a gigantic sign atop the Million Dollar Pier that positively dripped with neon. But in wartime, it no longer glistened in the night. Christmas lights were prohibited. Trolleys, jitneys and automobile lights were painted half black, and smoking was prohibited on the Boardwalk, streets and in automobiles. The glow even went out of families, whose sons either enlisted or answered the draft to serve in the nation's armed services.

The fear of German submarines near the Naughty Queen's shores was less fairy tale than reality: German U-boats had torpedoed tankers on the East Coast — some just a few miles north and south of Atlantic City — during World War I, and the federal government had every expectation that attempts would be made again to disable shipping.

Precautions against attacks from the sea also included Coast Guard patrols and the formation of civil-defense teams to alert islanders to the potential danger of walking on the beach at night.

According to Margate's Herb Gaskill, the bodies of German sailors washed up on the beach, but civil-defense personnel decided to withhold that information for fear of alarming residents. There also were rumors that German soldiers had landed in small boats at the Inlet. Dressed in civilian garb, they were said to have gone to the movies.

New Year's Eve Frolic
500 CLUB
$7.50: Tax Included
N? 545

GOOD FOR ONE ADMISSION
to the
500 CLUB
New Year's Eve Frolic
Famous Acts of Screen, Stage, Radio and TV
Novelties, Noisemakers, etc.
Including Breakfast
PRICE $7.50: Tax Included
N? 545

It was in these times that Skinny D'Amato sought sole ownership of the 500 Café, which also was called the 500 Club. By the time the club became the hottest spot in town, it was known by a jazzy nickname, the "Five." A mere joint when Skinny took over, he built the Five into a world-class club hung with the signed photographs of the stars who performed, and hobnobbed, there.

Upon entering the front bar, one could not help but to notice booths with zebra-striped fabric lining the walls. Looking back toward the entrance, there was a waterfall with lights and plants, which created a garden ambience. The bar and bar stools were ebony, and the carpet was burgundy with black swirls.

Beyond that first bar was a smaller one, where patrons waited to enter the famed Vermilion Room and see some of the century's most famous performers. True to its name, the room had burgundy velvet-flocked wallpaper, which was accented with white sconces. White linen tablecloths fluttered against ebony chairs. Dishes bearing the insignia "the 500" matched the vermilion theme with pale burgundy borders.

After Barr's departure, Skinny held a twenty-five percent interest in the club, as did partner Irving Wolfe of Washington, D.C.; Mario DiFonzo of Wilmington, Delaware, owned the remaining fifty percent.

A highly individualistic man, Skinny had something of a mystique about him. It may have been a shield to cover his lack of formal education or whatever vulnerabilities he harbored. As such, his strengths, and maybe his fears, too, made him the ultimate host. He was a natural politician, knowing intuitively that a handshake sealed not only a deal, but also a promise, that power could be built upon helping others find their place or a job, and that it was always good business to slip a "bone" to those less fortunate.

Skinny's handsome looks and suave manner worked like a magnet for women. It's arguable that no one before or since has looked better in a tuxedo. He had presence, and when he entered a room, people were drawn to him.

Men considered Skinny "a man's man." He was emulated in many ways, and men lived vicariously through him. Adding to his appeal was his code of ethics: He disliked men who used vulgarities in front of women, and he disregarded a person's creed or race. He had a penchant for attracting celebrities, but he also didn't forget those people who no longer were part of the "in" crowd. When Skinny became manager of the 500 Café, he invited the fallen-from-favor Nucky and Flossie to spend Saturday nights there.

No doubt about it, Skinny was a shrewd man. He sized up people, their moves, their actions and their ulterior motives. He was so smooth about it, though — ever the gracious nightclub impresario exuding glamour and excitement.

In the early 1940s, Skinny called upon his sister Patty and her husband, Philadelphia businessman Sammy Cohen, for a loan. Three days later, they handed Skinny forty thousand dollars in cash, in essence the keys to the store. It was his chance to realize his dream.

Skinny prepared to celebrate his sole ownership of the club with a gala opening, but, having just bought the place, he had no money left over to purchase the quantities of liquor he hoped to sell. His friend

Nucky Johnson, while at the height of his political career in 1930. His signature carnation, usually red, is white here, perhaps so that it would stand out in the black and white photograph. Above, a plate from the Silver Slipper Club, about 1929.

Flossie Osbeck, Nucky's future wife, on left, and Hazel Scott on the beach in the 1930s.

Willie Pastore and Skinny D'Amato, age 25, walk the Boardwalk in 1933.

Willie D'Amato, bottom, right, with pals in front of Skinny's cigar store in 1928.

Phil Barr, in the late 1930s, first owner of the 500 Club.

Al Wohlman with the 500 Club Chorus in 1934.

Flossie and friends.   *Flossie and Nucky at the 500 Club.*

Phil Barr, left, top row, in the late 1930s.

Scrip issued in 1933, signed by Enoch L. Johnson.

Men feeding worthless scrip into a furnace in the late 1930s.

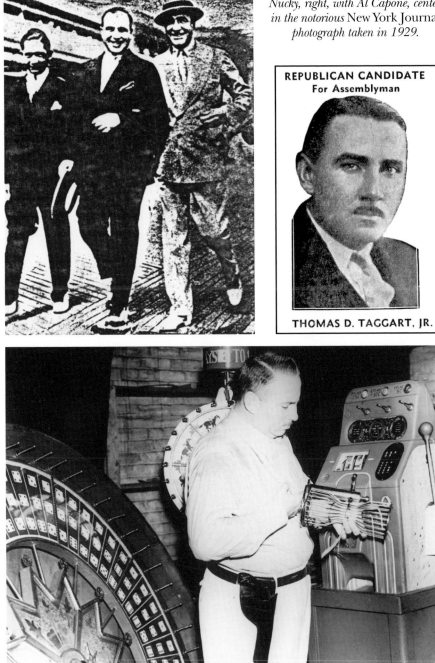

Nucky, right, with Al Capone, center, in the notorious New York Journal *photograph taken in 1929.*

REPUBLICAN CANDIDATE
For Assemblyman

THOMAS D. TAGGART, JR.

Mayor Thomas "Two-Gun" Taggart in 1942, and, above, right, in a campaign poster.

A 1940s advertisement for the famous yacht-shaped bar.

Bath & Turf Club, a Chinese restaurant and gambling joint.

When in Atlantic City visit . . .

BABETTE'S

Famous for

Charcoal Broiled Steaks
Chops and Sea Food

★

Dinner and Supper
Floor Shows

visit BABS YACHT BAR

Mississippi and Pacific Aves.   Atlantic City, N. J.

Skinny and Willie D'Amato with Skinny's terrier.

Willie in 1930, left, at age eighteen. Grace Anselmo, right, at age seventeen, before her marriage to Willie.

An officer measures a woman's bathing suit in the 1940s, as a crowd looks on.

The kindhearted and hardworking "Six-Foot Lizzie," 1930s.

An elderly Nucky Johnson applauding contestants in Miss America Pageant in the 1950s.

Harry James Orchestra with Frank Sinatra, bottom row, third from right, in 1939.

Skinny, his uncle Mike D'Amato and band leader Harry James.

Frank Sinatra and Skinny D'Amato.

From right: Noro Morales, World War II heartthrob Betty Grable, her husband Harry James, Irving Wolfe and Skinny D'Amato, between two unidentifed guests.

Cocktails anyone? The 500 Club lounge and its signature plate.

"Skinny loves celebrities": Joe E. Lewis and Jimmy Durante.

Joe E. Lewis, Skinny and Walter Winchell lean in for a confidential discussion.

From left, Skinny, Morris "Ding-a-ling" Cohen, Milton Berle, Jimmy Ceres, Jackie Gleason and an unidentified man are being ushered into a dining room by a waiter.

As usual, it's a crowded night at the Five, about 1940.

Down The Shore Publishing
P.O. Box 3100
Harvey Cedars, New Jersey 08008

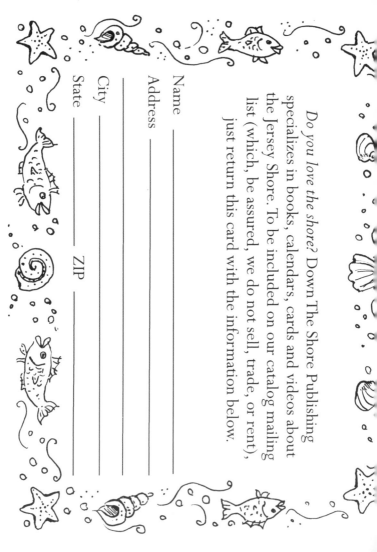

Do you love the shore? Down The Shore Publishing specializes in books, calendars, cards and videos about the Jersey Shore. To be included on our catalog mailing list (which, be assured, we do not sell, trade, or rent), just return this card with the information below.

Name _____

Address _____

City _____

State _____ ZIP _____

Recovering World War II soldiers on the Million Dollar Pier in 1945.

Troops marching past Haddon Hall when it was used as a hospital in 1942.

Emil "Willie" D'Amato, far right, seated, entertaining soldiers at the Five in 1944.

Blacks endured racial prejudice throughout the nation, but they were always welcome in the 500 Club; 1944.

Skinny D'Amato, Bettyjane Creamer and Mr. and Mrs. Bernard "Toots" Shor, 1940s.

Willie and Grace D'Amato, Bettyjane Creamer and Skinny, 1948.

Dean Martin, Skinny, Jerry Lewis and Morris "Ding-a-ling" Cohen onstage in 1946. Below, Dean and Jerry at the Five.

Dean Martin and Jerry Lewis flank Skinny onstage in 1946.

Celebrating Jimmy Durante's birthday; Skinny and Durante are in the center of the photograph.

The Red Hot Mama,
Sophie Tucker, and Skinny
in the 1950s.

Trolleys share the road with cars on Atlantic Avenue in 1950.

"Will you have a drink with me?" Skinny in the 1950s.

Skinny with his sister, Patty D'Amato Cohen, 1950s.

Joe E. Lewis, Senator Hap Farley, Bettyjane D'Amato, "Honey" Farley and Skinny in the 1950s.

From left: Peter Miller, T.T. Argenti, Willie D'Amato, Miskie Cohen, Kay Tito, Patty D'Amato Cohen, Ella Cohen, Grace D'Amato, Columbia D'Amato, Skinny D'Amato and Dick Bacharach.

Skinny, Bettyjane and Jack Benny in the 1950s.

Lee Wolfe, Joe DiMaggio, Skinny and Toots Shor in the 1950s.

Boxing at the 500 Club in 1950s.

Dean Martin, at right, ponders over the towering figure of 500 Club doorman Raymond "Seven-seven" Harris in 1954.

They're ALL stars: Joe DiMaggio, Frank Sinatra and Skinny.

A dreamy Marilyn Monroe seems to enjoy the ride as grand marshal at the Miss America Pageant in 1952

Chief photographer of Atlantic City Al Gold kisses Marilyn Monroe during the 1952 Miss America Pageant.

An advertisement for the 500 Club touts Frank Sinatra and Dean Martin.

Dean and Jerry backstage in 1952. They appeared at the Five every summer until 1956, when the duo dramatically split.

Colby Berenato sent him a cache of liquor, but to Skinny's horror, the booze was stolen. Skinny's brother, Willie, dashed out to buy two bottles of liquor, one scotch, one whiskey, and the club's doors opened. Throughout the evening, as the money came in, Willie ran to the liquor store and replenished supplies.

Conventioneers visiting the city and looking for a good time strolled Missouri Avenue, where they happened upon the club. They danced to radio music with the Naughty Queen's lovely princesses and had a great time. In all, a good crowd turned out for the celebration, and word spread that the 500 Club was a fun place to go.

The day after opening his club, Skinny purchased two cases of liquor. He hired a bartender from "Ali Baba and his Forty Thieves," his joking reference to the local bartenders union and its leader. One of his bartenders was a man named Louie Masucci. Louie was beloved for his gentleness and even temperament. But he had a brother, Fred, who was rather a different sort.

Fred Masucci was a wealthy man and a friend of Stumpy Orman's. He was known as much for his wealth as for his stinginess. When he went out to dinner and it came time to divide the check, he would excuse himself and go to the men's room until the danger of having to pay for the meal was over. Interestingly, when Louie found himself a bit short of cash, he called upon Stumpy for a loan, not Fred.

When he finally could afford it, Skinny added to the club's aura by hiring an orchestra and performers who were searching for their break in show business. He knew what his patrons wanted, he knew talent, and he knew how to sign it for his stage. It was exhilarating. Skinny finally was on his way up, and he knew that, too.

He was widening his circle of friends and influence as well. When autumn winds began buffeting the shore, Skinny would journey to New York City. There, he frequented restaurants and bars, including those owned by boxing great Jack Dempsey and entertainer Bernard "Toots" Shor. At Shor's place, where Damon Runyon hung out and wrote about the characters he met, Skinny met Joe DiMaggio, Frank Sinatra and other notables of the stage, screen and sports worlds.

During World War II, some five hundred thousand servicemen were stationed in Atlantic City, where they conducted drills on the Boardwalk, according to the book *Shore Chronicles*, Margaret Thomas Buchholz's compilation of travelers' diaries. The city's grand hotels became lodgings for some soldiers, hospitals for others.

Among the servicemen in the resort was baseball great Joe DiMaggio. The Yankee Clipper was thrilled in February 1945 to receive the transfer he had requested from Hawaii, according to *Joe DiMaggio: The Hero's Life*, by Richard Ben Cramer. Atlantic City held the spring training grounds for the New York Yankees, and it was close to New York, where DiMaggio's wife, actress Dorothy Arnold, and his three-year-old son, Joe Jr., were living. DiMaggio's marriage was in trouble at that point, and he had hopes — which were not realized — of saving it. When the Atlantic City transfer came through, DiMaggio's friends put

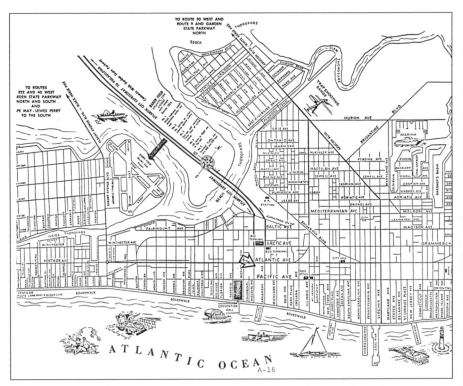

A map of Atlantic City with an arrow pointing to the 500 Club's location.

in a call to Sam Camarota, the owner of the Hialeah Club, asking him to take care of Joe.

"What am I going to do with Joe DiMaggio?" Camarota moaned. Then an idea came to him. "I've got it! I'll send him to Skinny. He likes celebrities."

Skinny liked DiMaggio all right. The baseball great stayed with Willie at his apartment, while Skinny built him a flat adjacent to his own quarters above the club.

Naturally, Skinny had a casino in the Garibaldi Club, next door to the 500 Club, where islanders and tourists found themselves in the company of some very swank people. Among the celebrity guests were Sinatra and orchestra leader Harry James and his wife, Betty Grable. Though an actress by trade, Grable is best known as the World War II pin-up girl whose shapely image gave morale-deprived soldiers so much to imagine. When the buxom Grable gambled at Skinny's casino, dealers purposely placed the dice at a distance from her in the hope of glimpsing her cleavage as she bent over.

Figuring the angles on Grable's game was not the dealers' biggest problem, however. The law was. One night, New Jersey State Police troopers raided the club, looking for the gaming room.

Gamblers and dealers scrambled to escape while Willie scooped up the cash. He stashed the money in a cloth bag, ran to the fire escape and climbed to the roof. The chase, the sound of dogs barking, and the fear of being caught, on top of the horror of possibly losing the day's receipts, were nearly overwhelming. Willie needed to hide, and quick. Looking around, he was dismayed. There was only one place to go, a chimney. Willie jumped into it, and he stayed there until the troopers had gone. Then, all sooty and cramped, he climbed out, handed Skinny the money, and went home to take a shower.

Beneath that chimney, the 500 Club was hot. It had a great show, good food, dancing until dawn — and one could almost always see a celebrity mingling in the crowd or at Skinny's table. The club and Skinny became famous throughout the United States. Big-name entertainers who came to play places like the Steel Pier would unwind later at Skinny's place, and they often would perform there gratis. Jackie Gleason was among those who had fun at the club, doing his bits for the crowd alongside the house musicians.

Of course, most patrons were less illustrious, and some even were more or less notorious. Among them were racketeers who frequented the 500 Club during the week with their "broads." On weekends, though, they were portraits of holy matrimony with their wives.

Skinny now had success, fame and a growing income. He also had a mistress whom he adored: Gambling. At times he would hole up in a Manhattan hotel with a suite of rooms to indulge his passion for running games of poker and gin. His clientele included wealthy businessmen and big gamblers who sought to challenge him and win. But they deluded themselves. They were up against the "master shuffler."

Beneath his charming manner, Skinny knew the odds, percentages and strategies of his card games. He was a card counter, which meant he remembered which cards had been played. He also was an excellent observer who correctly read his opponents' hand movements and other body language, allowing them to give themselves away. On top of all that, he was a great bluffer. There was no doubt about it, Skinny was no cheater. He just knew how to play the game — in every sense.

S kinny had an eye for talent, and young entertainers were thrilled to be given an opportunity to perform at the 500 Club. This mutually beneficial situation resulted in Skinny offering his patrons unknown performers who later became nationally and internationally famous.

In 1946, Skinny hired a scrawny, little-known comedian from New York. The man had worked the Borscht Belt in New York's Catskill Mountains, but outside of that venue, the name Jerry Lewis didn't mean much to many people. So Skinny paid him one hundred and fifty dollars a week. He also hired a velvet-voiced singer from Ohio. Dean Martin had established himself in nightclubs, so Skinny paid him seven hundred dollars a week. Martin was a carefree, easygoing man; Lewis was intense, sentimental and a worrier.

Skinny was not overly impressed with either performer individually, but, by chance, he got the idea that they could work together. As Lewis told it on an *Arts & Entertainment Network* biography of the Rat Pack, he was bombing onstage and got the hook. While he was packing his things in his dressing room, Martin went onstage and made a quip about Lewis's performance. Still offstage, Lewis heard the remark and answered back. The audience found the repartee hilarious, and Skinny took notice. He hired Martin and Lewis as a duo, and one of the most enduring, and famous, comedy partnerships was formed.

The new team went down to the beach and put on a drowning act for beachgoers. The crowd that gathered around them thought they were wildly funny and laughed at their antics. Lewis called out to them: "If you think we're dying now, you ought to see us at the 500 Club." The audience roared and applauded.

The two men later sat inside a pavilion on the Boardwalk and discussed possible comic bits. According to Jimmy McCullough, the 500 Club's publicist, the only thing Martin and Lewis could come up with at first was their friendship.

When they did arrive at the 500 Club, the new comedy duo startled customers and waiters by squirting them with water pistols. The patrons howled with laughter. They loved Martin and Lewis; applause resounded throughout the club. Later, the comics shook hands with those who had been such good sports. McCullough recalled that entertainer Sophie Tucker, the Red Hot Mama, had seen Martin and Lewis and compared them to Abbott and Costello.

Club ownership played to all of Skinny's strengths as a businessman, congenial host and *bon vivant*. He knew which table to give to whom, and he always made sure that his serving staff checked with him before handing guests such as judges, lawyers and politicians their tabs. His generosity may have been driven less by altruism than by self-interest and a need to be admired, but no one was keeping score. People came to the 500 Club to have a good time, and Skinny made sure they did. He was a man who was loved and revered a great deal more than he was disliked.

In 1947, Frank Sinatra performed at "Skinny's saloon," as he
liked to call it. Frank was down
about his career and popularity,
which both seemed to have
foundered. Skinny reassured
Frank that his career would re-
vive, and he gave the singer a handsome gold
wristwatch as a token of their friendship.

On one occasion when Sinatra was in his slump, he showed up in
Atlantic City despondent and broke. He had lost his recording and
movie contracts, and he told Skinny and Joe DiMaggio he was going to
meet his second wife, actress Ava Gardner, in Africa, where she was
filming *Mogambo* with Clark Gable.

Ava had sent Sinatra money for airfare, but he wanted to buy her
a present. He asked DiMaggio for a thousand dollars. DiMaggio refused, and Sinatra went to the men's room, deeply hurt. In Sinatra's
absence, DiMaggio commented that he would not lend money to a has-
been.

Skinny then asked DiMaggio if he would loan him one thousand
dollars. DiMaggio glanced around the prosperous club, figured Skinny
was good for it and promptly peeled off and handed him the bills. When
Sinatra returned from the men's room, Skinny slipped him the cash.
Sinatra left soon afterward for Africa, where we must imagine Ava was
the recipient of a lovely gift.

When Sinatra was a guest at the 500 Club, he would mingle in the
club's front lounge. There, in a mannerly and humble way, he would
ask waiters and waitresses for a drink or something to eat.

Skinny observed this interchange, and he took his friend aside.

"Frank," Skinny lectured, "important men don't ask, they order."

Frank nodded. He had learned an important lesson.

Two years later, on June 4, 1949, Skinny, 41, and a local model,
Bettyjane Creamer, 24, were married in a ceremony performed by At-

lantic City Mayor Joseph Altman at his home.

A stunning platinum blonde, Bettyjane was the only child of Edythe and Frank Creamer. Bettyjane had had rheumatic fever as a child, which caused her already devoted parents to coddle and pamper her even more. Skinny and Bettyjane came from two different worlds; she was the center of her parents' universe, and Skinny had been on his own since the age of fifteen.

The couple's wedding reception was held in the Vermilion Room at the 500 Club, and it was the social event of the year. Some 600 guests attended the lavish affair, in which strolling violinists weaved through the room. Large vases holding roses, baby's breath and other flowers adorned each table, and swans cut from ice were placed at each end of a buffet table filled with appetizers. Guests later sat down for a celebratory meal of filet mignon.

D uring the winter months, Skinny and Bettyjane headed south to Florida's Miami Beach. Skinny held court at the Fontainebleau Hotel, where he played host to big gamblers in private cabanas. Gin was the game, head to head, and baseball player Leo Durocher often brought players to the table.

Skinny's reputation as a great card player was well-established, and it led to challenges from others who thought their skills were superior to his. They would boast, and then they would lose. On one occasion, Skinny played poker in an all-night session and won one million dollars, which was considered a fortune in the fifties.

The vanquished challenger circled the room in a frenzy, distraught and crying out in despair."

"I've lost everything. My family will suffer," he lamented. "I'm gonna end it all."

Skinny pushed the man's money and notes away from him.

"Take your money back," he told the man, "but promise me you'll never gamble again. You're out of your league."

The story of Skinny's big win and bigger compassion spread up the coast and reached gambling quarters in Philadelphia, New York City, Washington, D.C., and, of course, Atlantic City.

Back in Atlantic City, Skinny held regular card games in the back of the club or in some fashionable hotel. Players were not terribly concerned about raids because, while they always were a possibility, Skinny had narrowed the odds somewhat with police payoffs.

During those wild and exciting days, Skinny and Bettyjane had a family. Their daughter Paulajane was followed by a second daughter, Cathy, and a son, Angelo. Willie and his wife, Grace, also had three children, sons Paul and Emil, and daughter Lisa.

As Skinny's fame and influence grew, many people infringed upon his name and popularity. He heard that he had nieces, nephews and cousins in Manhattan, Florida, Las Vegas and Los Angeles. With his typically dry wit, he scoffed at all of these so-called relatives, stating he had enough family that he knew.

Skinny and Bettyjane raised their family in a luxurious house in the exclusive St. Leonard's Tract section of Ventnor. The contemporary-style home had a front porch that ran the width of the house. Inside, the décor was white with orange (Sinatra's favorite color) carpeting. The spacious living room held contemporary furniture, with beige and orange draperies and a marble fireplace. French doors led out onto the lawn. During the summer, an orange awning provided shade.

The Sinatra theme was repeated in the kitchen, where orange Formica countertops complemented dark wood cabinets. The table overlooked a large yard and garden. In the dining room, crystal chandeliers reflected and sparkled in mirrors. The first floor of the house also had a huge den, powder room, maid's room and bath. Upstairs, Skinny and Bettyjane had his and hers bathrooms — his was black ceramic, hers white — and there were four other bedrooms, each with an adjoining bath.

One Christmas Eve, Skinny and Bettyjane entertained one hundred and fifty friends and notables at their home. At midnight, silence prevailed as Frank Sinatra and Dean Martin called to exchange holiday greetings with their pal. The hush over the house became a rush of whispers that further enhanced Skinny's reputation.

As he became more prominent, Skinny looked West, but he thought East. He saw that Las Vegas, Nevada, had sixteen million visitors a year, and he fervently wanted to bring legalized gambling, and the millions of tourists and dollars that would come with it, to Atlantic City. In 1954, he made his proposal, but the politicians nixed it. Their thinking, in part, was that gambling would bring more of the wrong kind of people — mobsters, hustlers and prostitutes, among others — to the resort. And so Skinny's vision would have to wait another two decades, until the city was so desperately gasping for life that the notion of gambling would begin to look very good to the politicians.

Skinny continued to run his nightclub, with nationally known headliners such as Joe E. Lewis; Vic Damone; Eartha Kitt; Jack E. Leonard; Jimmy Durante; Liberace, along with his piano, candelabra and brother George; Zsa Zsa Gabor; Al Martino; Toni Arden; Jayne Mansfield; Betty Hutton; Xavier Cugat, with his Chihuahua; Abbe Lane; Tony Martin; Milton Berle; Fran Warren; Sophie Tucker; Sammy Davis Jr. with the Will Mastin Trio; Martha Raye; Jackie Miles; Nat King Cole; Kitty Kallen; Dean Martin and Jerry Lewis; and, of course, the one and only Sinatra.

Sinatra's career had revived, and when he sang, 500 Club patrons were mesmerized by his performance and their proximity to him. Reservations for his engagements came from all over the United States, as well as Canada and even Europe. There was never an empty seat in the house, and in fact, people also stood along the walls.

As club manager, Willie saw the stars onstage, and in human form. He recalled singer and pianist Nat King Cole as perhaps the most gentlemanly of all the performers who played the 500 Club. Cole was classy and courteous, treating everyone with respect. He drove his own car and arrived without an entourage.

Willie also remembered the night Edward G. Robinson, the great actor and a well-educated man, came into the club. He wanted to meet Sinatra's friend Skinny. Robinson was alone, so Willie sat with him to keep him company while they waited for Skinny to finish a card game.

Robinson spoke Italian to a baffled Willie, who did not understand the language at all, except for the bad words.

Because Skinny's club was the place to go, ex-husbands and ex-wives often called ahead to prevent embarrassing interludes. When they forgot, it was up to management to intervene. A near miss resulted one evening when Willie greeted and seated Elizabeth Taylor and her husband, Mike Todd. Knowing that Taylor's first husband was in the club, Willie then rushed off to find Skinny, who exclaimed, "Nicky Hilton's waiting for me. I'll get rid of him. Keep them entertained."

Entertainers had many and varied requests, but none surprised Willie as much as the one made by Jayne Mansfield. It was five o'clock on a Sunday morning when she approached him and whispered: "Please take me to church."

Willie looked askance at her. It was five in the morning, and he wanted to get home. He offered a compromise, which she accepted. Willie led the lovely actress to his rusted and dented car. He wondered if she would turn her nose up at it, but she was gracious. They drove to a shrine at Our Lady Star of the Sea Church on California and Atlantic avenues and knelt in prayer. Willie then drove her back to her hotel and went home. Shortly thereafter, she died in an automobile accident, and Willie recalled with sorrow the warm, charming and beautiful girl.

With the constant threat of raids by law enforcers who were not on the graft payroll, gamblers found they needed to mix caution and creativity. But sometimes even the best plans suffered bad luck.

A flunky was assigned to the Atlantic City Race Course, given horses to bet on, and told to "play late" before the race went off. He was allocated ten thousand dollars, which he wagered over a period of three weeks and lost. Thus, he established himself as a bettor who played late and did not win.

The man was now instructed to return to the track and bet on a certain horse in the seventh race. That bet would follow the normal play-late-and-lose pattern. But the man was told to bet one hundred thousand dollars in the first race as well. That was a fixed race, and the man's boss was looking for a big payoff, in addition to recouping his ten thousand dollars from the previous three weeks.

Told to look at his boss's window for the number of the horse he was supposed to play, the man glanced up on his way to the track and saw the numeral "1." Unfortunately, the man misread the number because the window molding obscured the top of the numeral "7." As arranged, the seven horse came in first, and away went the boss's hundred grand. Presumably, the luckless gambler went away — and if he was smart, far away — too.

In 1950, a curious scourge overtook Atlantic City in the form of four young policemen. Local wags dubbed the officers the Four Horsemen in a sneering reference to the biblical Four Horsemen of the Apocalypse. Driving black patrol cars instead of horses, they brought war, famine, pestilence and near death to illegal gambling as they raided the Naughty Queen's betting parlors and brothels.

The four officers were Jack Portock, a veteran wounded in World War II and the father of six children; Fred Warlich, the leader, who served as secretary to the police chief; Francis Gribbin, a handsome, well-built man with black hair; and William "Big Six" Shepperson, a young officer with eight children.

Islanders did not consider these local sons local heroes, and the officers' zeal did not arise from any noble desire to better the city they served. Rather, they simply wanted a raise. The men earned fifty-two dollars a week, and any order for an increase had to come from Hap Farley, who ultimately controlled city and county jobs. That Farley had remained neutral in the matter was an affront to the men, who considered neutrality a negative position.

Believing that Farley had the power to increase their salaries, the Four Horsemen took a relentless stand, ironically, to do their jobs. This created chaos for politicians and islanders alike.

The Naughty Queen's subjects were divided on the issue, and those on the side of the administration thwarted the Four Horsemen's efforts. Their wives received threatening telephone calls, and they encountered one difficulty after another.

When a numbers operator conveniently filed charges of extortion against the four, they were suspended from the force pending an investigation. The officers were exonerated on the extortion charge, but their problems did not end. A charge of civil disobedience hung over their heads, and they were forced to resign from the police department.

Firemen and policemen were outraged at Farley's subsequent meeting with city officials, who determined police and firefighters would receive a bonus of two hundred dollars a year. The average police officer's salary was two thousand nine hundred and fifty dollars per year, and two hundred dollars already was their usual yearly bonus.

In 1951, U.S. Senator Estes Kefauver, chairman of the Special Committee to Investigate Organized Crime on Interstate Commerce, was looking into corruption in Atlantic City. Warlich, the Four Horsemen's leader, testified in 1954 before Kefauver's committee in Washington, D.C., that Farley's influence and power were all-encompassing in Atlantic County, and that Herman "Stumpy" Orman was the real power behind Farley.

Warlich's allegations against Farley and Orman could not be proved. The Naughty Queen snickered at the folly of those who would challenge her and smiled once again upon her favorite sons and illicit activities.

It was also in 1954 that Dean Martin and Jerry Lewis had booked a return engagement at the 500 Club. The zany pair were famous now, and the city buzzed with excitement over their appearance. On the first night of their engagement, one thousand reservations had to be turned away for the duo, who only recently had been unknown. But Martin and Lewis played for ten nights, and thus gave their fans a chance to see them perform.

The first time Martin and Lewis had played the 500 Club, they had worked cheap. But their first movie had grossed ten million dollars, and they now commanded a huge salary.

1946

1954

The Five Hundred Club requests the pleasure of your company at a buffet supper in celebration of the Eighth Anniversary of DEAN MARTIN and JERRY LEWIS as the World's Greatest Comedy Team on the Evening of Thursday the Fifteenth of July at half after eleven o'clock The Vermilion Room 500 CLUB Atlantic City, New Jersey

Martin and Lewis had virtually nothing in common in their tastes and temperaments. After work, Dean went home and watched television, while Jerry worked in his film laboratory. A sentimentalist, Jerry performed with a photograph of his first wife, Patty, and his sons in his pocket. Patty Palmer sang with Jimmy Dorsey and his orchestra and had been well-established as a star by the time she married Jerry.

With the galaxy of stars who performed at the club, Skinny reached his zenith. He was famous, his club was famous, and even his headwaiters achieved some certain fame. Barry Sloane, maitre d'hotel, worked at the Five during the summer and at the Latin Casino in Cherry Hill, New Jersey, during the winter. Rags Gordon worked in Florida during the winter, but he returned to the 500 Club every summer as maitre d'. He was a Dean Martin look-alike and was popular among the nightclub circuit.

Adolph Marks, a maitre d' from a Philadelphia establishment, liked to hang around the club, where he enjoyed the atmosphere, the characters and the celebrities. When he declared himself a headwaiter, Skinny called Willie aside.

"Who the hell hired him?" Skinny asked.

"He hired himself," Willie answered. "He's been helping out. I'll tell him he has to go."

"No, let's see how he does," Skinny said.

Skinny could not find it in his heart to fire any employee, and if Willie did, Skinny rehired them after listening to their sob stories.

Like Nucky, Skinny was well-known for his generosity and support of charitable causes. During the Christmas season, he would send the 500 Club show to a mental hospital on the Atlantic County mainland in Northfield. The show also went

A publication of the 500 Club.

to the Betty Bacharach Home in Longport and to the Children's Seashore House in Atlantic City. In addition, Skinny permitted charitable organizations to use the club's Vermilion Room for fund-raisers, and sharp-eyed Five patrons could not help but to notice that amid all the high-style nightlife, Skinny kept a donation box in the club. Proceeds from that box went to St. Michael's Roman Catholic Church on North Mississippi Avenue, where Skinny and Willie's parents had been parishioners.

Atlantic City and its institutions bestowed many accolades upon Skinny, who had done his utmost to succeed in business and promote the Queen of Resorts as well. He was proclaimed Atlantic City's Honorary Mayor in 1969, and the *Atlantic City Press* honored him as Man of the Year in 1981.

As Skinny had hoped and predicted, Sinatra's career had found its way back into the spotlight. When Sinatra won an Academy Award for his portrayal of Maggio in *From Here to Eternity*, Skinny sent him a telegram:

"PER CENTO ANNI!" he wrote, saluting his friend and wishing him one hundred years of life and good health.

Sinatra was in Spain, filming *The Pride and the Passion* with Sophia Loren and Cary Grant, but Skinny anticipated some word from his friend. It was not immediate in coming, but eventually a telegram arrived: "How about the 23rd, 24th, 25th and 26 of July?" It was signed "El Dago." Skinny and Sinatra could tease each other about their shared Italian heritage, and they did so rather often, but no one else dared to join in.

In July, 1956, the acclaimed Sinatra arrived incognito at the club's garage in a beat-up, borrowed car driven by Mario Floriani, a sergeant for the Atlantic City Police Department who would later become police chief. Skinny, Bettyjane and a select group of friends greeted Sinatra, while children sneaked around for a glimpse of him. He took the time to speak to them and sign autographs, and they ran away jubilantly.

Stories have been told about Sinatra's petulance and temper. He did once overturn a card table holding a rum cake that was almost the size of the table. The cake had been made especially for him, but Sinatra ditched it because the smell of the oozing rum had nauseated him. But he was more kind than fiery, more respectful than not, and he was loyal to his friends.

At the club, elderly men and women who could not afford the price of a ticket to see Sinatra perform waved at him instead. They also tried to shake his hand, but the police shooed them away. Touched by their appreciation, Sinatra told the police to bring them inside to see his performance.

During his engagements, Sinatra added shows to accommodate his fans, who were enraptured with him and his sexy voice. Men stood on chairs, yelling and applauding, while women screamed his name, their faces aglow with love.

The last time Skinny brought enchantment, in the form of Sinatra, to Atlantic City was 1962. The anxious Queen poised herself for Sinatra's appearance and the flood of people who would come to see him. A sign outside the 500 Club heralded his arrival with an effervescent "He's Here!"

Sinatra acquired an interest in the Cal-Neva Lodge, a Lake Tahoe, Nevada, nightclub, hotel and casino in 1961, and he needed a casino manager. He turned to Skinny, who then began spending his summers in Nevada.

Back home in Atlantic City, Willie looked after Skinny's club. Skinny hired various managers, who sometimes became part-owners of the 500 Club. In that capacity, they were in a position to overrule Willie's decisions, which they occasionally did. But Skinny was shrewd, and he kept Willie in the club not only because Willie was his brother, but also because Willie was the only person he trusted.

"My brother creates monsters," Willie once said. "Their egos weigh them down. But when he gets mad, he brings them down to size."

Upon Skinny's return, he would curb the oversized managers/part-owners and run the club his way. Contrary to popular opinion, Willie was not a partner in the club's ownership. Willie's loyalty to his brother was admirable and true, and it was built upon a promise he made to their mother. Mary D'Amato died when she was only thirty-eight years old. On her deathbed, she told Willie to watch out for the family, especially Skinny.

There's no doubt Willie and Skinny were close, and had been so, all their lives. When Willie was fourteen years old, a neighborhood kid threw an open safety pin at him, and he lost the sight in one eye. Skinny wanted to go after the kid and avenge his baby brother, but Willie held him back. The two brothers sat down and wept together.

On one particular jaunt to the Cal-Neva lodge, Skinny encountered legal problems. He was accused of bribing an agent with a C-note. The adverse publicity, coupled with the involvement of Chicago mobster Sam Giancana, prompted Sinatra, and consequently Skinny, to abandon the venture. Thus, Skinny's summertime sojourns to Lake Tahoe ended.

FRANK SINATRA'S

Cal-Neva
LODGE

PAUL (SKINNY) D'AMATO

PHONE
702-831-0410

CRYSTAL BAY
LAKE TAHOE, NEVADA

Skinny didn't mind that result terribly, though, because he loved Atlantic City, where his life and character had grown and he had become well-established. He ruled the island's nights with great love, and in return, he received the affection of the Naughty Queen's subjects. He counted Frank Sinatra among his closest friends, and that relationship, in more ways than one, was worth its weight in gold. Sinatra performed gratis at Skinny's club, in exchange for first-class accommodations.

In January 1960, Skinny received a contract from Sinatra's lawyer. with the following stipulations:

> This agreement made and entered onto this 11th day of January, 1960, between PAUL D'AMATO and FRANK SINATRA, it is hereby understood and agreed as follows:

> That for and in consideration of the appearance of Frank Sinatra and the services to be performed by him at the "500 Club" in Atlantic City, New Jersey, that the said Paul D'Amato is to comply with certain conditions and requests of the said Frank Sinatra as follows: That the said Paul D'Amato is to arrange and obtain all necessary hotel accommodations with air-conditioned living quarters to be acceptable by Frank Sinatra for himself and for all members of his staff. That Frank Sinatra is not limited to the amount of members of his staff.

> That the said Paul D'Amato is to furnish and have available at all times six (6) charming and congenial (also well-bathed) ladies to function and administer their talents, attributes, and assets for the complete happiness of the said Frank Sinatra and the members of his staff.

> That the said Paul D'Amato agrees to use all his efforts to keep Mr. Toots Shor off of the premises of the "500 Club," and the premises where Frank Sinatra and his staff are domiciled during the period of his engagement, arrival and departure from Atlantic City.

> In witness thereof, we have hereunto set our hands and seals this 11th day of January 1960.

Skinny signed the document, but Sinatra did not. His lawyer scrolled a circle, a symbol some Jewish immigrants used to sign their names, and, in this case, a mark that could not be ascribed to his client. Sinatra loved to play jokes on Skinny, and Skinny was too busy laughing to take offense at his friend's zany sense of humor.

When Skinny returned from Lake Tahoe, he brought with him a valise containing five hundred thousand dollars. About a month after he got back, he was playing gin with some wise guys from Trenton, New Jersey. Willie caught the mobsters cheating, and when the card players took a break, Willie approached them. He was not the least bit intimidated by them.

"What the hell are you guys doing," he asked, "robbing him?"

"Willie," one responded, brushing him off, "your brother's a big boy. It's his problem, not yours. Besides he won't believe you."

"Yeah, sure," Willie mumbled as he walked away in disgust.

The mobsters were right. When Willie told Skinny about the cheating, Skinny dismissed Willie. He could not believe that anyone would dare to try to cheat him.

The wise guys and Skinny played cards all night, and Skinny lost the entire half million dollars. Willie winced at the waste, and the swindle.

Skinny, however, was nonchalant about his loss. It wasn't so bizarre — he won millions and lost millions. What was odd, though, was that Skinny's intuition had failed him. He had been unfailingly dead-on right about people, about the way they moved, about what lay behind their facial expressions, and about their ulterior motives.

Not surprisingly, rumors circulated that Skinny was involved with organized crime. His name took on a slight tarnish, but his power remained undiminished. Islanders still needed favors, and Skinny was dependable.

There was gossip at one point that the mob had offered Skinny the South Jersey territory. When asked about this, his quick, smart reply was: "I have South Jersey."

Thus, Skinny dismissed the rumors and the rumormongers, and he treated the wise guys with respect. Besides, they loved nightclubs, and that was good for business. Perhaps Skinny recalled club owner Dan Bastian's comment that hosting the Mafia is "like having the United States Army behind you."

With the sixties came changes that would profoundly affect American life in general, and Atlantic City specifically. Prosperity and the Jet Age allowed people to go farther away than Atlantic City, and they did. The Naughty Queen saw her convention business decline, and she was going down with it. Skinny's tourism axiom, "All we need is hot weather and Frank Sinatra," once so obvious, seemed a little less so now.

Yet celebrities still adorned the 500 Club, wanting to meet Sinatra's good friend Skinny. Among those stars were Burt Lancaster, who in the next decade would play a rather unsavory character looking for the right scam in the decayed resort in the film *Atlantic City*.

In 1967, thirty men arrived in Atlantic City from Palermo, Sicily, with their bodyguards. The entourage was escorted by Angelo Bruno, the so-called "Docile Don" and head of the South Philadelphia mob. The purpose of their meeting was to see the famous 500 Club, where Sinatra performed, and to hold a meeting.

None of the men spoke English, and Bruno communicated with them in Sicilian. Bruno ordered a private banquet room, with protective covers on two small windows. The waiter set the table with paper napkins, and when Skinny checked the room, he was furious.

"Those guys dine on fine china and use linen napkins," he said. "Change them right away. They'll get insulted."

The waiter shuddered, gathered up the paper napkins and replaced them with cloth napkins. For good measure, he shaped them into fans.

After dinner was served, the room was locked and bodyguards stood in front of the doorway. Skinny was not permitted to attend the meeting. Not that he would have wanted to! Anyway, he wouldn't have understood what they were saying.

The meeting lasted a few hours, and when the men emerged, Skinny took them on a tour of the club. He shook hands with them, and they thanked him for his hospitality.

Word spread about the notorious meeting, and the FBI tapped the club's telephones. Employees were warned and gave the bureau no rewards, instead treating the listening agents to stupid and silly remarks. The FBI also set up a surveillance site in the parking lot across the street from the club. During the few months it was in operation, club employees gamely waved to the cameras as they left work.

Skinny went about the business of expanding his interests. He opened the Beef and Beer, an intimate bistro that was connected to the club and specialized in roast beef sandwiches. It was there that islanders gathered after a movie to see the real-life cast of characters who came in to dine. No matter what was playing at the theater, the Beef and Beer was "the best show in town."

One evening a man sat alone, brooding, in the Beef and Beer. His face was etched with fury, his eyes dulled behind horn-rimmed glasses. Otherwise unremarkable with gray hair and a medium height and build, there was one striking characteristic about this man: A scar, faded but still visible, was cut into his forehead.

A waiter flagged Willie, telling him that the man appeared strange, off-center in some way. Willie approached the man and shook his hand.

"Cappy," Willie greeted the former Nucky Johnson minion. "How are you? How about a drink?"

"No, I'm waiting for one of your waitresses," the bitter man responded.

"Who?"

"She isn't going far," Cappy Hoffman said, without offering the woman's name. "I put sugar in her gas tank."

Willie gulped. He eyed the door, and the steps that led down into the restaurant.

"I'm going to kill her," Cappy stated with quiet reserve.

"Have a drink," Willie repeated.

"She took my money, now she doesn't want to see me."

"Don't do ..."

"There she is!" Cappy exclaimed.

He bent down, retrieved a baseball bat and chased after the woman with Willie in hot pursuit. The woman reached her car and locked herself in. Cappy pounded the car with the bat, inflicting dent after dent as the terrified waitress sat trapped inside. Willie struggled with Cappy for the bat, while the waitress escaped. Afterward, Willie led Cappy back into the restaurant and ordered a whisky for him and coffee for himself.

"Cappy, do you want to go back to jail and die there?" Willie asked.

Age had softened Cappy Hoffman's mean features, but Willie knew he was still a dangerous man. Yet Willie had the ability to soothe those who were tormented. In the end, Cappy thanked Willie and left quietly. He never came around the club or restaurant again, much to Willie's relief.

Willie was five-feet, eight inches tall, with a medium build, a pugilistic nose, brown hair and one brown eye and one blue eye. When he encountered dangerous people, he showed caution, but never fear. If chills ran through him, he never displayed any emotion. His even temper, compassion and fairness earned him respect. He was a devoted family man and a hard worker at the club, where just about anything could, and did, happen. Willie's favorite expression was his observation that "The whole world's nuts ... very few sane people."

Besides the 500 Club, islanders and visitors would patronize Harry the Hat's Restaurant. Located down the street from the club on Missouri Avenue, the jovial owner would greet his customers by singing "I'm Harry the Hat, I'm round and fat. That's why all the people come back ..."

At the corner of Missouri and Pacific avenues, Belle Barth, who was ahead of her time, performed at Le Bistro. Her vulgarity shocked many customers, but she also developed a following. Old-timers remember Le Bistro as the former Applegate's Tavern.

In July 1968, Dr. Bernard Barab, a local dentist, entered Atlantic City Hospital and saw a familiar face. He looked at the man, and looked again. It was Nucky all right. Nucky grinned. He was still his engaging self, despite Barab's observation that there was not a card, a flower or a plant sent to cheer him. Apparently, the Naughty Queen's subjects had forgotten him and the kindness and generosity he had shown to the less fortunate when he had been boss of the city.

Nucky was a black marketeer, no doubt, but he also had loved the Queen with all his heart. The Queen was fickle and opportunistic, however. She had no time for a has-been heartthrob. She had new men, full of energy and ideas, to keep her life exciting and fast. But she lacked the insight to see that like Nucky, she also would falter.

An aged and ailing Nucky was placed in a home for the elderly in Northfield, New Jersey, where he died on December 9, 1968. He was 85 years old. Flossie was at her husband's side.

"I love you, Baby," he told her.

"I love you, too," she wept.

Despite his criminal activities, Nucky still is praised today by some old-timers. They remember how much fun Atlantic City was back then and how safe it was for families. They most of all remember that Nucky's public-menace persona was balanced, to them, by the kind and thoughtful man who aided the poor.

One person recalled Frank Hague's assessment of Nucky: "He was a tall, striking man with a light in his eyes that made ordinary appraisals of the man seem petty."

Even the *Atlantic City Press*, which had chronicled his misdeeds, was charitable in the end:

> Nucky Johnson ruled Atlantic City in the manner of the Grande Seigneur. He was born to rule, he had flair, flamboyance and was politically amoral and ruthless. In another age, he could have been a baron on a hill or a Roman pro-consul ...

The newspaper had called Thomas "Two-Gun" Taggart a faithful servant, but his tactics had created extreme dissension among islanders. Nucky, however, had been the Naughty Queen's boss, her lover and her champion. He is remembered, legitimately, as a bootlegger, a pimp, a womanizer, a tax cheat and the leader of an illegal enterprise called Atlantic City. But he also must be credited with being among those whose vision allowed Atlantic City to claim, rightfully, the title Queen of Resorts.

Nineteen hundred sixty-eight was going to be a lousy year for Skinny. Even worse, it was going to be the turning point from which he would not recover, either personally or professionally.

That year, Skinny was charged with failure to file corporate taxes. He did not contest the charges, and in 1971, the 500 Club was allowed to remain open under receivership.

Skinny's friend Barry Kravitz organized a testimonial dinner on Skinny's behalf to boost his spirits and help defray his legal expenses. One thousand tickets were sold for one hundred dollars apiece, which raised a large sum of money, minus the cost of the meal, for Skinny. The dinner was held at the club, and there was not a vacant seat. Dolly Sinatra represented her son Frank.

Skinny had given Atlantic City — and the state and the country — so much, but he had never needed anyone's charity in return. Now that he did, he was stunned to see that people arrived from all over the nation. Helping Skinny was a *cause celebré*, and the outpouring of affection touched him deeply.

Never far from Skinny's thoughts was the idea of legalized gambling in Atlantic City, and how to make it happen. Of course government-sanctioned gaming would serve the interests of his business and personal devotion, but Skinny also ardently believed it could only benefit the city, too.

He read with interest on the subject, including an article Sidney Harris wrote in the 1970s for *The Philadelphia Inquirer*. The article quoted the English essayist, novelist, and critic Gilbert K. Chesterton: "A man has the right to bet what he has the right to lose. If he bets more, he is like an alcoholic who drinks more than he should." That was a position with which Skinny always had agreed.

The article also offered for debate the argument that "Legalized gambling would hurt mobsters" and further stated that absent legal control "... the authorities have simply augmented and entrenched the power of organized crime. Our hypocritical attitude toward gambling has done more to subvert the law in the United States than anything since the wretched Volstead Act." (The reference of course is to the Eighteenth Amendment to the U.S. Constitution, which Republican Andrew Volstead introduced in the House of Representatives in 1919 to prohibit the sale of liquor. Prohibition resulted in the booming black-market liquor trade that enriched many people, including Nucky Johnson, but supplied no tax revenue to the government.)

The Naughty Queen was abuzz with talk about legalized gambling, but there was little support in the Statehouse in Trenton for throwing the dice to revive the faded dowager. The Queen was once so polished, so elegant, so chic. But she now was so decrepit, with paint peeling like so many layers of pancake makeup to reveal the creases and pock marks of life lived to excess. Her businesses, hotels and homes were haggard or shuttered, her children were fleeing the island for better opportunities elsewhere, and her ocean washed only sand upon her sparsely visited beaches.

Skinny's financial problems grew worse as well. The fabulous acts he once had at the club now were accessible to the entire nation via television. The wondrous invention of TV was poison to the health and well-being of the 500 Club.

Despite the slump both the Queen and Skinny found themselves in, accolades and honors continued for the latter. The George A. Hamid Tent of the National Circus of Saints and Sinners "roasted" Skinny at his club. He was among the Queen's most notable personalities, and though never an elected official, Skinny, rightfully, had been dubbed "Mr. Atlantic City." His love for his hometown was indisputable, and when others abandoned and criticized the fallen Queen, he worked harder to enhance her image.

D evastating tragedy was about to strike Skinny and his family. Bettyjane had become ill, suffering from petit mal seizures. The cause was found to be an inoperable brain aneurysm. She died in 1972 at age forty-six. Islanders were shocked as they mourned the beautiful, vibrant woman known as "Mrs. Skinny."

In addition to her husband, Bettyjane left behind her three children. Paulajane was then twenty-two years old, Cathy was twenty and Angelo was thirteen. Flowers and condolence cards and telegrams came from both the East Coast and the West. The family was particularly touched by a lavish floral arrangement that Frank Sinatra and his mother had sent.

A nyone who's ever tried to build sand castles on the beach knows the awful reality that they can never last. Either the ocean will wash them away when the tide comes in, or, if they are built beyond the high-tide line, the wind and the rain will get them. The elements will always win your dream. You get to keep your memories. If you cherish those thoughts of what once was, of what you built with your own hands, they will bring you pain and pleasure in equal amounts.

On June 10, 1973, Skinny's castle was washed in a flood. But the fire came first.

The massive blaze started in a dressing room near the Vermilion Room. Skinny had rented the room out for disco dancing, and men who smoked there had a habit of dumping live cigarettes into the trashcan. One smoldered there, near the boxes of 500 Club matches that had been piled nearby on a table.

Skinny was sipping coffee in the club when his staff ran to tell him the draperies had caught fire. It already was too late. Within moments, the club was an inferno that devoured everything Skinny had built.

Smoky clouds filled the sky and drew throngs to the horrific scene. People stood before the fire, mesmerized, helpless, as they watched the ravaging of a favorite night spot and piece of Americana. Some wept. Others shook their heads in sad disbelief.

Walls collapsed like carelessly tossed pieces of paper. The roof caved in. Firefighters flooded the seething flames with arcs of water that cascaded into the debris. Muddy soot slopped over the tables and chairs. Twisted metal hung monstrously above the grotesque scene.

Finally, the flames were subdued, the sirens were silent. The 500 Club was gone. All that remained of the structure were broken walls, overarching metal and charred beams. Eerily, singed and soggy parts of the fabled stage in the Vermilion Room still stood, and a gigantic photograph of Frank Sinatra still hung in its accustomed place, barely touched by fire or water.

Skinny was stunned beyond shock. He had buried his wife not even a year before. Now, not only had years of his work been turned to ashes in mere hours, but he also had almost lost his son. Angelo had been asleep in the apartment above the club and barely escaped the flames.

Skinny's friends, family and club patrons surrounded him. But their words of condolence were lost somewhere between the wind and the sound of crashing waves. The loss was overwhelming to Skinny. *The Press* newspaper reported that a radio newsman at the fire scene asked Skinny how much his building was worth.

"It's the value of my life. I don't know how much that is," Skinny answered.

Curiosity seekers from various parts of New Jersey, as well as from Philadelphia and New York, converged on the resort to see the disaster and pay their respects. The fire was big news, and reporters descended upon the scene, too. They questioned Skinny about the value of his club and whether he had insurance. They also knew there was that tax matter, and they wondered if arson was involved. But Skinny loved his business and never would have torched it. Besides, his child was on the premises at the time of the fire.

As it turned out, Skinny did not have enough insurance to compensate him for the loss. He had four hundred thousand dollars worth of coverage, but his club, restaurants and bars were worth at least two million dollars. Tears welled in his eyes.

"It's my life," he lamented, "the value of a lifetime."

Skinny went home. His mind was muddled as friends embraced him and tried to console him. They told him he would have to rebuild, and that Atlantic City needed the 500 Club. One hundred and fifty people were out of work as a result of the fire. Skinny merely nodded.

Reporters and customers hounded Skinny about rebuilding the club, but the reality of its demise was setting in for Skinny. Sure, he could make another club, he could even do it on the very spot where his first one had been, but he could never rebuild the floors that had felt Sinatra's feet, or the walls that had held his voice. Without the real 500 Club, what did Skinny really have? Sensing this, reporters asked Skinny if it would ever be the same.

"No," Skinny said, "it's a new world of entertainment. I don't think the club could make it today. It would be too expensive to build."

Skinny was out of a job, and so was his brother. Willie became "the prince of Atlantic Avenue", which is the Naughty Queen's main thoroughfare. He worked in the city's traffic division, painting lines on the street and putting up signs. He lost his nightclub pallor and was greeted daily by islanders calling out: "Hi Willie!"

There was a seemingly endless proclamation of his name, and he responded to well-wishers by name, too. He was far less famous than Skinny beyond the Naughty Queen's borders, but no less beloved inside her domain.

Legalized gambling still dominated Skinny's thoughts and conversations, maybe even more so now that he didn't have the club anymore. His philosophy about gambling reflected his beliefs about life.

"The breaks are everything," he would say. "It's the roll of the dice, the flip of a coin, the cut of the cards, the turn of the wheel, or whatever. You have to be in the right place at the right time."

Skinny waited for the lucky flip of a coin or cut of the cards at home in Ventnor. He played gin and poker, or solitaire when he lacked a partner, and took the plethora of telephone calls that helped console him.

Skinny still could draw a crowd, and islanders continued to honor him at fund-raising dinners for their favorite charities. A man at one such dinner yelled out: "You're the 'godfather' of us all," which brought resounding laughter to the room.

In 1974, Skinny predicted the Naughty Queen, with her smeared lipstick and sagging stockings, could become a paradise again. Local business people and politicians agreed. The drive for legalized gambling had never been stronger, and it had become a national topic. Nevada, then the only state that sanctioned gambling, was uneasy about having a rival on the East Coast. The issue also raised the age-old debate over whether gambling was harmless entertainment that brought governments easy money or soul-stealing sin.

Mike Wallace of CBS television's *60 Minutes* interviewed Republican New Jersey Representative Millicent Fenwick, Atlantic City Mayor Jay Bradway, the Reverend Vincent DiPasquale of Holy Spirit Roman Catholic Church in the city's Inlet section, local businessman Gary Malumut and Skinny.

At one point, DiPasquale, who opposed bringing gambling to the city, told Wallace: "The prophet Jeremiah in the Old Testament says a lot of things that I'm saying. He said it about Jerusalem instead of Atlantic City. If you read one of the chapters about false prophets —"

"Are all those men false prophets?" Wallace interjected.

"They're developing the concept of false prophets by which they're telling people their salvation is going to be found in money and the development of gambling in the city."

"Are you preaching the Gospel, according to Father Vince?" Wallace queried.

"No, I'm teaching the Gospel, according to Jesus Christ, I hope."

Mayor Bradway framed his pro-gambling viewpoint to Wallace in human terms:

"What gambling will do for the population, in total, including the black population," he said, "is create stability of jobs."

Gary Malamut also favored gambling, and he was emphatic:

"I've seen casinos in Europe, the Caribbean, Curacao, Portugal, Nevada, and I've seen the clientele these resorts attract. Those are affluent, high-income people who have disposable income to spend, not only in the casinos, but on retail sales, in restaurants, hotels and on consumer items. They are usually happy and say, 'I had a great vacation.' "

Fenwick was equally emphatic, though of the opposite opinion.

"This is out of this world!" she declared.

"Isn't it nice to get 'out of this world' every now and then?" Wallace asked.

"Not if your family's going to pay for it. We've got to stick to what works," she responded.

The final interview was with Skinny.

"Skinny," Wallace asked, "Can the state run a gambling operation?"

"I don't think there's any way that the state can," Skinny replied. "You can't win without credit. Nobody's going to carry fifty thousand dollars or a hundred thousand dollars. The state's not going to give anybody fifty or a hundred thousand dollars credit."

"But the private operator will?" Wallace asked.

"The private operator will do this," Skinny affirmed.

Ultimately, and as usual on the subject of gambling, Skinny was correct.

In his book *Hostage to Fortune: Atlantic City and Casino Gambling*, author Michael Pollock notes that the excitement in Atlantic City over a November 1974 statewide constitutional referendum that would permit casino gambling was not shared by voters throughout New Jersey. For one thing, there was the link between organized crime and gambling. For another, that ballot referendum would have allowed gambling throughout New Jersey, and people didn't want slot machines for neighbors.

The pro-gambling forces regrouped, and in 1976 they presented another referendum that limited gambling to Atlantic City. In addition to that significant change, Pollock notes, gambling revenue was dedicated to programs for senior citizens.

Thus, the fear of rampant casinos was allayed, and the powerful senior-citizen vote was secured. That 1976 was a presidential election year also meant a higher voter turnout could be expected than in an "off-year" election, such as in 1974. Not leaving anything to chance, however, the Committee to Rebuild Atlantic City (CRAC) was formed, and it outspent its anti-gambling opposition by a 60-to-1 margin. As a result, Pollock wrote, New Jersey voters approved casino gambling by a 200,000-vote margin.

Prominent business people, professionals and ordinary working people had come together and hired a consultant, Sanford Weiner, to lobby for gambling's passage. A master strategist and veteran of many political races, Weiner put together a comprehensive advertising and public relations campaign that included the effective use of local and state politicians' glib skills. State Senator Joseph McGahn, whose attorney brother Patrick had brought Weiner into the effort, and Steven Perskie, a lawyer who later became a senator, judge and then head of the state Casino Control Commission, spoke eloquently in defense of legalized gambling. Skinny participated and gave his views, as well.

When casino gambling was legalized, the Naughty Queen and her subjects rejoiced. The Queen would get her needed facelift and new palaces. The media descended upon Atlantic City, the slum by the sea that now was so full of hope.

In 1978, the Queen's first new palace, Resorts International Hotel Casino opened in what had been Haddon Hall. Old hotels were razed to make way for new ones, so that there are 12 casino hotels in Atlantic City: Resorts; Tropicana Casino and Resort; Showboat Casino Hotel; Ballys Atlantic City; Caesars Atlantic City; Claridge Casino Hotel; Atlantic City Hilton Casino Resort; Sands Hotel Casino; Harrah's Casino Hotel; Trump Marina Casino Hotel; Trump's Plaza Casino Hotel; and Trump Taj Mahal Casino Resort. Another 2,010-room palace, The Borgata, is on the way.

Like their predecessors, the gaming areas are smoky, but there the resemblance ends. What had been small, back-room, and classy in a clandestine sort of way, now is big, and loud, with people, swirling color schemes, bright lights and clanging bells. But the Naughty Queen is not unpleased with her pulsating palaces. She may have traded sexy memories for cheap thrills, but the new arrangement has brought her money, jobs and rejuvenation.

Skinny received many offers to build a casino hotel on Missouri Avenue, directly across from where the 500 Club once stood. He also had an offer to be involved in the Shangri-La Motor Inn, which was to be built at the foot of the Atlantic City Expressway. Skinny declined, and that casino property never came to be.

One reason for Skinny's reluctance was that financing was prohibitive. He would need "angels," as he had in the past, when those with the largest purses had the honor and privilege of sitting at his table on New Year's Eve. Often he had needed a fast fifty thousand dollars, and his angels were always there to supply him with the money.

But Skinny wasn't twenty years old, or even thirty or forty. He was almost seventy. It was 1976, and the city and the business were different. He may even have tired of wheeling and dealing his way through life. The hustle takes energy, and Skinny was running low in that department.

Skinny had been one of the Queen's favorites, but she had moved on without him. He now held court in his bedroom, where he was recovering from a heart attack. He was catheterized but had been declared an unfit candidate for open-heart surgery.

He still had spunk, though. In 1979, a friend told him that *The New York Times* reported his death. Skinny scoffed at that "news," declaring he was very much alive and well and living in Ventnor. Those who remembered Skinny from the 500 Club visited and paid their respects to him at his home. But above Skinny's house, up higher on the island, the Naughty Queen's streets were busy with gamblers looking for the big win, and entertainers looking for the big time.

Frank Sinatra was back in town after some years of absence. His name was legend, his voice was still magic, and people came in droves to see his casino-showroom performances.

One evening when Sinatra was performing at Resorts, Sophia Loren was in the audience with Sinatra's friend, Jilly Rizzo. At four in the morning, Sinatra told Jilly and Pat Henry, a comedian and opening act for Sinatra, to bring Sophia to visit Skinny.

Skinny, as almost anyone would be at that hour, was wearing his pajamas and a robe when he greeted his unexpected guests. Laughing, he knew Sinatra was responsible for the visit. After a delightful conversation, he thanked his company for visiting him and made sure he kissed Sophia Loren as they said *ciao*.

Sinatra liked to play pranks on his pal Skinny, but their friendship was deep and enduring. Onstage in Atlantic City, Sinatra never failed to mention that Skinny was responsible for bringing casino gambling there. Among Skinny's other friends with whom he had tearful reunions in later years were Dean Martin and Jerry Lewis, Danny Thomas, Sammy Davis Jr. and Eddie Fisher.

In 1978, a *Courier-Post* newspaper headline described Skinny as a "fat cat before gambling vote." After noting the names of Skinny's famous friends, reporter Ron Avery went on to say that "Perhaps the most intriguing aspect of this very unique man is the fact that D'Amato made a bundle of cash from 'casino' gambling in Atlantic City years before the people of New Jersey voted on casinos."

"Atlantic City was Las Vegas," Skinny told Avery. "This town was wide open. There were crap games all over town. People came here from all over the country to gamble."

In that article, Skinny also reflected upon his youth and how he had run card games in the back room of his store.

"I did good. I got a bigger joint, and then a bigger joint and then a bigger joint," he said.

"Look, everybody knew it," Skinny continued. "The State Police knew about it. The FBI knew. The whole country was like that."

Sinatra, seated, with Mannie Sachs and Skinny, 1950s.

Skinny, Dean Martin and two young girls who had edged to the front of the crowd to watch Martin write his name in cement in front of the 500 Club in 1954.

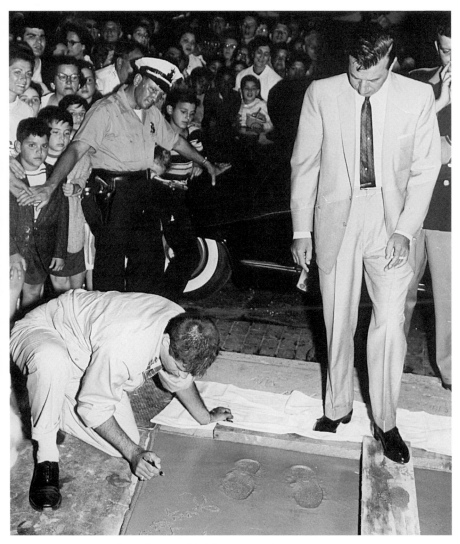

Jerry Lewis adds his name to the cement, too.

The city provided a police escort to the famous performers at the Five who were often besieged by admirers. Dean with an officer in the 1950s.

Skinny poses with convalescing youngsters at the Children's Seashore House.

George Liberace, Patty D'Amato Cohen and Liberace in the greenroom of the 500 Club. The brothers performed together at the club in the 1950s.

Sammy Davis Jr. performs with the 500 Club band.

Skinny with Lee Meriwether, Miss America 1955.

Skinny, center, as he hosts the Press Club of Atlantic City at the Five.

Before entering the Vermilion Room, Donald O'Connor, an unidentified clubgoer, Swifty Morgan, Skinny, Keely Smith, George Raft, unidentified man and Louie Prima pose for a photograph at the bar.

Milton Berle and Sammy Davis Jr. are at home onstage at the Five.

Celebrating Bettyjane and Skinny's tenth anniversary at the club are: Grace and Willie D'Amato and John Scanny in front; Mr. and Mrs. Mario Ruberto, Marie D'Amato Ravielli, Joseph Ravielli and Columbia D'Amato.

Like so many of the era's popular entertainers, the charismatic Vic Damone performs at the 500 Club.

185

Milton Berle with James McCullough, Willie D'Amato and Ralph Sloss in 1958.

Enjoying an evening out: from left, Preston Robert Tisch, Mrs. and Mr. Earl Wilson, James McCullough, Mrs. Laurence Tisch, and an unidentified man. The Tisch family operated the Traymore Hotel.

Jack "Colby" Berenato with Skinny. Before Skinny became involved in the 500 Club, he had managed the casino at Luigi's Bar and Restaurant, which was owned by Berenato.

Frank Sinatra's albums are on display with a smiling doorman.

Sinatra poses with Patty D'Amato Cohen in the greenroom, and at left, with Skinny, who is receiving the 1959 Sinatra Award.

Souvenir publicity shots commemorate Sinatra and the 500 Club.

Sinatra's photo hung above the club entrance a decade before his triumphant return to the Five in the 1960s, as advertised on the billboard pictured below.

They're here, too ... Crowds inside and outside the 500 Club, hoping for a glimpse of Sinatra.

Skinny, Bettyjane, Judge Angelo Malandra, Felix Bocchicchio and others arrive with Sinatra.

Sinatra takes the stage at the 500 Club.

192

Sinatra addresses Mike Todd, standing behind Mannie Sachs, recording executive from Columbia Records sitting across from Leo Durocher and his wife, actress Laraine Day.

Sinatra turns to address his accompanist, to the amusement of the packed house.

The hushed crowd drinks in Sinatra's melodies.

Marty and Dolly Sinatra at the 500 Club. Below, their son Frank thrills the crowd.

Sinatra's last performance at the 500 Club, in August 1962, accompanied by Dean Martin. Below, Frank Sinatra and the 500 Club Chorus.

The McGuire Sisters at the 500 Club in the 1960s.

Rare event! Skinny dances the twist with Phyllis McGuire, who was the girlfriend of mobster Sam Giancana.

Skinny poses with South Carolina Senator Ernest Fritz Hollings and singer Patti Page. The photograph is inscribed:

Skinny - this is when we both hit the big time.

— Fritz Hollings

Love from me, too!

— Patti Page

Nat King Cole, Willie D'Amato and Louis "Looch" Calabrese in the 1960s.

Bettyjane, Jerry Lewis, Skinny and Dean Martin on "The Today Show," broadcast from the 500 Club in 1960.

Al Martino and Skinny pose below a poster of Sophie Tucker.

Willie kneels alongside Zsa Zsa Gabor, top left, as she signs her name in concrete at the entrance to the Five in the 1960s.

Look at those jewels! Zsa Zsa Gabor and Skinny, above, and left, in the Five's greenroom, with James McCullough.

Jayne Mansfield presses her toes into the cement in front of the club, as Willie D'Amato and husband Mickey Hargitay assist.

Frank Sinatra Jr., Willie and a customer at the Five.

Cohen family and friends, clockwise from left: Lou Cohen, Rose Cohen, Kay Tito, Vic Damone, Patty D'Amato Cohen, Sammy Cohen, Skinny, Al Martino, Lenora Slaughter, Joey Bishop and Joe Frasetto.

Skinny speaks to John F. Kennedy in 1960, an acquaintance founded on their ties to Frank Sinatra. Skinny had used his gambling connections in Greenbriar County, West Virginia, to finagle the votes Kennedy needed to win the state that year.

Democratic delegates fill Convention Hall to support Lyndon B. Johnson's presidential nomination in 1964.

Club Harlem and Larry Steele's Smart Affairs brought fame and recognition to talented black performers such as Sarah Vaughn, Ella Fitzgerald, Count Basie, Ray Charles, Ethel Waters and many more. The club attracted music enthusiasts of all races.

Hap Farley, Judge Angelo Malandra, for whom Skinny's son is named, and Skinny at the D'Amato home in Ventnor. Below, Enzo Stuarti, singer at the Five, and Skinny at a fund-raiser in the 1970s.

Skinny received public recognition for his role in the evolution of Atlantic City.

Below, a telegram from Sinatra to Skinny and Bettyjane.

"*Speech!*" *Skinny with Judge Angelo Malandra, Police Chief Mario Floriani and Mike Segal at one of the many benefits held in Skinny's honor. Below, friends Dean Martin, Skinny and Sinatra.*

Firefighters poised above the roof of the doomed 500 Club, above.

A crowd gathers as the fire burns, left, and clouds of smoke billow behind the club.

A photograph of Sinatra and part of the stage in the

Vermilion Room were all that remained after the fire.

Frank and Barbara Sinatra attended the dedication of an Atlantic City Medical Center wing bearing the singer's name. Sinatra raised six hundred thousand dollars for the wing in a 1978 benefit concert.

In 1980, the original star-signed cement slabs were moved from the club entrance to Skinny's home in Ventnor. Stars, like Danny Thomas, shown here, continued to preserve their names in Skinny's back yard.

Sinatra attends a party held in Skinny's honor by the Hebrew Academy of Atlantic County, May 1981.

Newsman and Skinny friend Sonny Schwartz hands Sinatra a yarmulke at the Hebrew Academy.

Sinatra kisses Skinny, left, and lights his cigarette.

_____

Sinatra, the Reverend George Riley of Villanova University and Skinny.

Jerry Lewis onstage with Sinatra at the Hebrew Academy.

Below, photograph from an article about Skinny honored with the prestigious "Man of the Year" award in 1981.

A night for "Skinny"

"Skinny" D'Amato (right) who will be honored tomorrow night with a prestigious "Man of the Year" award is shown here with the top names that made his 500 Club the "in" spot of yesteryear. Joe "The Yankee Clipper" DiMaggio (left), Walter Winchell and George Raft.

William Weinberger, president of Bally's Park Place, Skinny and Billy Martin, manager of the Yankees, at a sports dinner held at Bally's in 1983.

Below, Emil D'Amato, Willie's son, an unidentified friend, Billy Martin, Mickey Mantle, Skinny, Willie Mays and Bill Dougall, president of the Claridge Hotel Casino.

Skinny celebrates his 75th birthday at the Golden Nugget with, clockwise from left, Sinatra, Jilly Rizzo, Reds Barone and Dean Martin.

A testimonial dinner for Skinny, center, drew one thousand guests.

Skinny and City Commissioner Joseph Pasquale at the section of Missouri Avenue renamed 500 Club Lane.

The Mass of Christian Burial

Paul E. "Skinny" D'Amato
June 9, 1984
One O'Clock
St. Michael's
Roman Catholic Church
10 S. Mississippi Avenue
Atlantic City, New Jersey

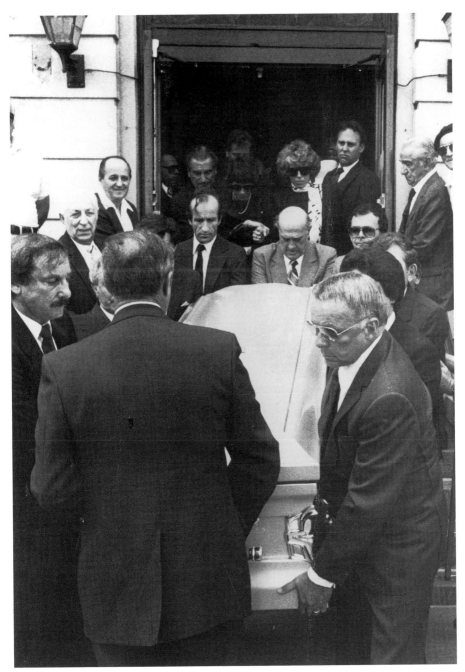

Frank Sinatra acts as a pallbearer at Skinny's funeral.

Sinatra mourns D'Amato

By JULIE BUSBY
Of the Courier-Post

ATLANTIC CITY — When the black hearse pulled up in front of St. Michael's Roman Catholic Church on Mississippi Avenue, the two bag ladies moved off the church's concrete steps out of respect.

They walked across the street to an abandoned brick building and stood in the shade.

There, they joined two dozen onlookers, attired in Bermuda shorts or wild print tent dresses, who had gathered to catch a final glimpse of Paul E. "Skinny" D'Amato and his funeral entourage.

Mr. D'Amato, the owner of the famed 500 Club from the 1930s until it closed in 1972, was often called Mr. Atlantic City or Mr. Nightclub. He died of a heart attack last Tuesday at age 75.

More than 300 relatives and friends came to mourn yesterday afternoon.

As the midday heat helped spread a thick haze over the crumbling neighborhood, the crowd waited for the pallbearers to arrive.

For 45 minutes, the sun baked the roof of the hearse that contained Mr. D'Amato's silver casket.

Men dressed in dark suits and sunglasses paced on the church steps, flashing pinky rings and black and gold cigarette cases.

Their female companions timidly approached the hearse, kissed their finger tips and then touched the vehicle.

Please see SINATRA, Page 8A

Courier-Post photo by Al Schell

Frank Sinatra attends funeral Mass In Atlantic City yesterday for Paul E. 'Skinny' D'Amato, known to many as Mr. Atlantic City, who died Tuesday. Sinatra is flanked by D'Amato's daughters, Kathy D'Amato (left) and Paula Jane D'Amato at the rites in St. Michael's Roman Catholic Church.

Final goodbye
Frank Sinatra (right) leads other pallbearers as they carry the casket of Paul E. 'Skinny' D'Amato out of St. Michael's Roman Catholic Church in Atlantic City, following a funeral Mass for the owner of the famed 500 Club. Mr. D'Amato was buried in Mays Landing.

Courier-Post photo by Al Schell

Sinatra attends final rites for Paul 'Skinny' D'Amato

Continued from Page 1A

And at one point an Atlantic City police car raced up and dropped off three young altar boys who moments earlier had been whisked to another section of the city for white robes.

Shortly after 1 p.m., seven pallbearers finally took Mr. D'Amato's casket from the hearse and carried it just inside the main doors of the church.

At that moment an eighth pallbearer, entertainer Frank Sinatra, accompanied by two bodyguards, walked from the front of the church down the aisle toward the casket.

When he reached the casket he paused, sighed and then helped carry it to the altar. The choir sang "Inherit the Kingdom."

Although the four-page funeral program handed out to each participant listed Sinatra as one of 10 pallbearers, the crowd had been wary.

They didn't believe he really would attend.

But earlier, to avoid crowds, Sinatra had arrived in a silver limousine, slipped in a back door of the church and remained in the vestry until the funeral services began.

Sinatra's affiliation with Mr. D'Amato began in the early 1950s. At a time when the famous crooner's singing career was on the wane, he appeared at the 500 Club. Later, when his entertainment fortunes improved, he returned to the club eight times and performed for free.

In the early 1960s, Sinatra purchased a casino in Lake Tahoe, Nev., and Mr. D'Amato managed it. Federal agents shut the club for allowing known gangsters to be privileged customers.

At yesterday's funeral, Sinatra sat in the right front pew between Mr. D'Amato's two daughters, Kathy and Paula Jane.

The Rev. George Riley delivered the eulogy.

"People, who need people, are the luckiest people in the world . . . Many of us here came within the magic circle of Paul 'Skinny' D'Amato. We are indeed among the luckiest people in the world," he said.

"He preached and taught us the realities of life, from the womb to the tomb . . . . He was the man for all seasons, even though most us of knew he preferred the summer and the nighttime.

"Skinny was a real student of the living. His summa cum laude was from the streets. He did not dazzle. He only tried to deliver.

"The gold and glitter of Broadway to the simple man on the street, they all came to him. His heart, indeed, never failed anybody."

Later, Mr. D'Amato's nephew, Emil, spoke.

"Someone earlier said, 'There dies a legend,'" he said. "A legend did not die. An era died. His legend lives on. His life seemed to be a life of the longest running craps game. On June 5, he sevened out. When you left, Skinny, the game shut down for good."

After the funeral, Mr. D'Amato was buried in Holy Cross Cemetery in Mays Landing.

Sinatra left immediately after the church services. He kissed both of Mr. D'Amato's daughters and then returned to New York, where he performed at Carnegie Hall last night.

The procession of more than 100 cars that traveled to the cemetery crawled past Missouri Avenue, the site of the 500 Club.

At that club, entertainers such as Dean Martin, Jerry Lewis, Sammy Davis Jr., Liberace and Nat King Cole once ruled the stage.

In the 1930s, Mr. D'Amato recounted in a 1978 interview, the club was a front for a sophisticated gambling operation. He later toned down the gaming aspect and converted the 500 Club into a restaurant.

As the fortunes of Atlantic City diminished, the club also suffered.

The showroom of the 500 Club closed in 1972. In 1973, the building burned down.

Mr. D'Amato then retired to his home in neighboring Ventnor, where each day he drank 40 cups of coffee, smoked five packs of cigarettes, watched television and phoned friends.

After legitimate casino gambling appeared in Atlantic City the 500 Club block became a parking lot and the site of a gas station and White Tower restaurant.

A section of Missouri Avenue was renamed 500 Club Lane.

"I knew Skinny for 40 years. He was the greatest, he helped everybody. He was helping people to the day he died," recalled mourner Danny Lucera, 74, at the funeral. Lucera was a 500 Club bandleader during the 1960s.

"He always called me 'The Champ.' I tell you, there'll never be an Atlantic City like the old days. And now, Atlantic City will never be the same now without Skinny. He was truly the greatest."

Skinny had received offers of six figures for permission to write his biography, but he turned them down. His loyalty would not allow him to sell out his friends with stories of their humanity in the face of the Five's temptations. Of Sinatra he was particularly fond, and no amount of money could entice Skinny to speak ill of him.

"Sinatra is the greatest," Skinny recalled. "Nobody knows all the good things he has done. I've seen him go out in the evening with ten thousand dollars in his pocket and give it all away by the end of the night."

One wonders if Sinatra emulated Skinny or if Skinny emulated Sinatra. Skinny, too, had been known to go out on the town in New York and Philadelphia, picking up the tab for all the patrons in night-clubs and restaurants, and spending ten thousand dollars himself in an evening.

Sinatra's petulance has been well-documented, but Skinny told Avery about the Sinatra who also was a good sport who could laugh at himself. Skinny once threw a cream pie at Ol' Blue Eyes in a restaurant. He did not miss.

"He loved it," Skinny said.

Ironically, Skinny, who had lobbied so long to bring legalized gambling to Atlantic City, had no plans either to own or patronize the Queen's new gaming houses. Resplendent with blackjack, craps, baccarat, slot machines, wheels of fortune and roulette, the casinos did not tempt Skinny one bit.

He had not envisioned colossal buildings, but rather small, intimate casinos, a place where families and businesses would reside and thrive. But homes were razed to make way for the behemoth gaming palaces, and those who could moved to mainland suburbs.

For his part, Skinny had no plans to be seen in the casinos. He preferred cards. But he did think Atlantic City would be a success.

"I don't know what I'll do," he told Avery. "... I never saved. I spent it as fast as I got it."

But Skinny liked to talk about gambling, and he was willing to share. In an interview with Michael Checchio, a reporter for *The Press of Atlantic*

City, the "master shuffler" offered some advice to gambling novices.

The first thing a person should do, Skinny suggested, is to watch for a while to get the hang of the game and the system. When ready to play, those new to gambling should start at a blackjack table because that game gives a slight edge to players. Of course, Skinny never wavered on what he considered the most important rule of all: Don't play more money than you mind losing.

"You can start with one dollar," he added, "and in fact, if you're lucky, you can play all night with one dollar."

When the first casino hotel had opened, *News World* interviewed Skinny.

"It's going to be a gold mine," he predicted correctly. "In seven to ten years, Atlantic City will eclipse Las Vegas. We have the finest beaches in the country and a great climate."

Atlantic City has not eclipsed Las Vegas, but it has done rather well after a slow start at urban renewal and casino-industry downturns mirroring the national economy.

In the early years of legalized gambling, Atlantic City looked more like two cities: The rich one along the Boardwalk lined the ocean and was studded with opulent casino hotels; the poor one was one block back off the "boards" and constituted much of the rest of the Queen's land area. The national media had a lot to say about legalized gambling's failure as a cure for social ills, but those news organizations have been noticeably silent since the experiment started having some success.

S inatra had once come to Atlantic City with a broken career, and a broken spirit. Not so in October 1978. He arrived in triumph, to the gasps and delight of the Naughty Queen's latest court, to perform a benefit for Atlantic City Medical Center.

The men and women who gathered in Convention Hall for Sinatra's appearance wore formal attire, and they felt great pride for their city and adopted son. In return, Sinatra sang for ninety minutes and raised six hundred thousand dollars for the wing that bears his name.

"It's one of the most beautiful evenings that I have ever spent in Atlantic City," said Dr. Joseph Stella, chairman of the hospital event's organizing committee. "I'm on top of the world."

Edward Knight, Ph.D., the hospital's president, and William Weinberger, president of Bally's Park Place, later presented Sinatra with a picture of the hospital that showed the subject of the benefit, a new section to be called the Frank Sinatra Wing. The singer and his wife, Barbara, were delighted with the presentation.

Skinny sat at ringside with his daughters. His complexion appeared pasty and haggard, but he answered the questions reporters posed. He would always be notable because he was Skinny, but he would always be news because he was Sinatra's good friend.

At a reunion in 1980 with Dean Martin and Sinatra, Skinny became a lifetime honorary member of the Frank Sinatra Society of New York. He had been a member of the International Frank Sinatra Society for many years. At that event, Sinatra called Skinny the "Ziegfeld of saloon keepers" and a living legend. He also commented on the years he had played Skinny's club.

"I had more fun working that little saloon than anywhere else I've worked," he said.

In May 1981, the Hebrew Academy of Atlantic County honored Skinny at a black-tie school fund-raiser that was held at the International Hotel in Atlantic City. Naturally, Sinatra, who was performing at Resorts International, was invited. There was awe when he arrived. The doors of the hotel parted, and the singer entered with his bodyguards, his grin lighting up the room. He embraced Skinny and sat next to him.

Jerry Lewis arrived later and joined them, and all eyes turned also to a big screen, where Danny Thomas and Dean Martin expressed their congratulations to Skinny.

Skinny was used to crowds, but he wasn't used to speaking in front of large audiences. On that night, though, he gathered his courage.

"I would like to thank Rabbi Krauss and the members of the Hebrew Academy for giving me this great honor. You all know, of course, that I have an Italian background, which I'm very proud of, but many of you know that I also have a Jewish background," Skinny said. "My brother-in-law is Jewish, and I have Jewish nieces and nephews. I've walked down the aisle of a synagogue as best man for my close friend, Sonny Schwartz, and my years in the nightclub business have brought me close to the people of the Jewish faith.

"My life has been one in which I have never chosen a friend because of color or religion, but I will say that Jewish friendships have been an important part of my life," he continued. "To all of you here tonight, Jews, Italians or whatever, thanks a million for just being here and sharing this very happy event with me."

Applause resounded throughout the room and tears slid down Skinny's face. He turned toward Sinatra, "You're my brother."

Willie's ears perked up, and he grinned from ear to ear. Despite the fact that he and Skinny had been close for many years, Skinny never praised him. Throughout the years, Willie had been proud of Skinny's unbridled success, his fame and his power. Willie's loyalty to his big brother had never wavered. Now, in front of all those dignitaries, Skinny finally was expressing his affection.

"Do you believe it? He's talking about me," Willie said to his wife.

Pained, I shook my head. "No, he means Sinatra."

Disappointment clouded Willie's face. He gulped and regained his composure as he left the affair with his sons, Paul and Emil, daughter, Lisa, and daughter-in-law, Sandi.

Organizations honored Skinny because he always drew a great crowd, and an Italian-American organization poured accolades upon this favorite son. At one event, Skinny was presented with a street sign that read 500 CLUB LANE to mark a renamed section of Missouri Avenue where the club once stood. (This sign can be seen by those who look closely when crossing Atlantic Avenue and traveling toward Pacific Avenue after exiting the Atlantic City Expressway.) It was at that affair that Skinny acknowledged Willie and his sister Patty for the first time.

In his last years, Skinny was retired, but he still continued the card games he so loved. A myriad of players would come from Baltimore, Washington, D.C., Philadelphia and New York. They often played in the penthouse at the Howard Johnson Hotel (now Caesars Atlantic City). But on other occasions when Skinny played host to small games at his home, he sometimes would get a call — just like old times — to be careful.

Skinny seldom rode past the place where his club once stood. The former ultimate destination is now a parking lot, a place to leave your car so you can be somewhere else. That piece of land, not far from the spot where he was born on the same street, was where Skinny's wildest dreams had been realized, and then burned to the ground. During the fifties and sixties, he had been the personification of the Naughty Queen's soul, imperfect, yes, but fun, generous and larger than life.

"The town was wide open," he would say, "and my club was the Shore's best bet."

Skinny knew that progress cannot be halted. Times change, and people either adapt or are lost in the grand shuffle. But islanders still solicited Skinny; even though he had taken himself out of play, they had not. They called him day and night:

"Skinny, lend me a thousand or maybe possibly, two ..."

"Skinny, I've written a song, perfect for Sinatra ..."

"Skinny, I'm a reporter. Can you get me an interview with Sinatra, or can you give me information about you and Sinatra in the old days?"

Skinny had an inherent yearning for public adulation, but his friendship with Sinatra was sacrosanct and off-limits to the public.

In December 1983, Dean Martin joined Sinatra at the Golden Nugget casino hotel to celebrate Skinny's seventy-fifth birthday. Despite Skinny's elation at the reunion, he was tired. Age, years of smoking and his late nights were taking their toll on the tough and gutsy entrepreneur. Who could have known that birthday celebration would be his last?

On Tuesday, June 5, 1984, Skinny D'Amato suffered his second heart attack. Complaining of chest pains just before one-thirty in the morning, he was taken to Atlantic City Medical Center. Skinny died there, a few hours later, at five forty-five, his usual bedtime, noted Schwartz, his close friend and a columnist for *The Press* newspaper. Skinny left behind his three children, a granddaughter, Devon, his brother, Willie, his sister, Patty, and numerous nieces and nephews.

In death, as in life, Skinny's private moments were public events. Scores of local dignitaries and islanders paid their respects at Skinny's viewing in St. Michael's Church. On June 9, Atlantic City police officers roped off an area outside the church for crowd control following Skinny's funeral. Islanders speculated about which celebrities might attend the funeral Mass, and curiosity seekers gathered beyond the cordon. Any celebrity, it seemed, would suffice.

Fittingly, Frank Sinatra was one of Skinny's pallbearers. He had been performing in New York City, and whispers spread throughout the church that he had flown in by helicopter and requested time alone with Skinny. Mourners kept a respectful distance from Sinatra. When he took his place in the church, it was with Skinny's family.

A lovely floral replica of the 500 Club stood beside Skinny's casket, but more poignant still was the singularly loving act of his children, who placed a deck of cards and a pair of dice in their father's pockets.

The Reverend George Riley of Villanova University, who had officiated at Farley's funeral, assisted in the Mass and extolled Skinny as a realist.

He was "a student of the living, a summa cum laude of the streets," an account in the *Sunday Press* of Atlantic City quotes Riley as telling the 300 mourners. "He did not try to dazzle, only hoped to deliver. The love of friends was, indeed, his reward this side of heaven."

Riley paused for a few seconds before continuing: "In the broad stream of life, of birth and of death, there are always a chosen few people who, by their deeds, their character, their lifestyle, their charisma, set a standard of human excellence for the rest of us to emulate and follow."

Mourners nodded.

Skinny, he said, "was the man for all seasons under the sun, even though most of us knew that he preferred the evenings."

When the subdued laughter died down, Riley grinned and then took note of Skinny's humorous, and astute, assessments of people. If he met someone who was tight with a dollar, he would say "that guy has glue in his pockets," and if someone was conceited, he would comment, "that guy couldn't run for dog catcher."

Willie beamed with pride as his oldest son, Paul, named for the uncle they were eulogizing, went to the altar and read from the Book of Wisdom. When his second son, Emil, stood at the altar preparing to speak, Willie looked at his wife. A double dose of pride overcame them.

"This morning a friend came up to me and said, 'There died a legend.' I said 'No, an era has ended, but the legend lives on,'" Emil D'Amato began. "Some people called him Skinny, some called him father, some called him brother, some called him uncle, but they all called him! They called him in the morning, they called him in the afternoon, and they called him in the evening. No matter what time of the day or night, they called him, and asked for this or that. When Skinny began his career, he rolled the 'dice of life.' When he died, he 'sevened out,' and the game was over."

The mourners burst out laughing. Skinny himself would have enjoyed his eulogy. He later was entombed in a mausoleum at Holy Cross Cemetery in Mays Landing, New Jersey.

With his brother gone, Willie, "the prince of Atlantic Avenue", retired to his "castle" in Margate and told his wife the stories he once had declined to relate about the bawdy, golden days of Atlantic City.

On May 28, 1990, Willie died of a heart attack. Fifteen hundred islanders paid their respects to his family. People recalled his gentle-

VENTNOR TAG SALE

PAUL "SKINNY" D'AMATO ESTATE SALE

Memorabilia
Photographs
Furniture
Clothing
Etc.

Friday & Saturday
January 10th & 11th
10am-6pm

12 S. Suffolk Avenue

CASH ONLY

ness, humility and, especially, his pride in his children's accomplishments. Besides his wife, he left three children and five grandchildren, Alexa, Ava and Ashley D'Amato and Adam and Jason Neustadter.

As cars streamed from the Blessed Sacrament Church in Margate, where he and his wife were parishioners, a police officer remarked: "His funeral is bigger than Hap Farley or Skinny's."

Epilogue

Legalized gambling has brought new luster to the Naughty Queen's jewels. In her renewed prosperity, she glows with the facelifts that new money has bought for her. And though she still trades on her reputation as a good time for all, her wicked, bawdy and glamorous proclivities have been subdued. She has lost her spontaneity in the trade-off, too.

But she stood to lose more without the casino gambling that finally rescued her. And truth be told, she is happy with her new palaces, resoundingly so. Their gaudiness suits her, as does their expense and decorators' touches. She adores the money they bring in, as well as the stretch limousines that carry important people and big-time gamblers to her shores.

Maturity has brought her respectability, and the confidence to name her price outright. She's come a long way from the Nucky Johnson graftathon and from those days when Boardwalk auction houses planted shills in the crowd to bid against tourists on furniture, paintings and jewelry.

Of course, there is crime still in Atlantic City, some petty, some horrible. There is illegal gambling, and prostitution, too. But these illegal enterprises do not exist so openly anymore. Their operators fear retribution now because the police have a better idea of which side they are on, and public opinion has swung against racketeers. People like Nucky Johnson and Hap Farley succeeded because they were wise enough to include everyone and make sure they all got something. But people since then have learned to take care of themselves.

And so has the Queen.

She has found a measure of protection in the state government of New Jersey, and closer to home, two mayors, James L. Usry and James Whelan.

The Queen's turnaround didn't happen right away, and for a long time it looked like it might not happen at all. Atlantic City made national news as a place where the promise of legalized gambling failed to deliver, where casino operators came in like con artists and took whatever they could without giving more than they had to back. Atlantic City became something of an embarrassing joke, too, because with all the elaborate precautions the state had taken to keep undesirables and their influence out of the resort's gambling industry, it overlooked the open door to the office of Mayor Michael Matthews.

The Pollock book, *Hostage to Fortune: Atlantic City and Casino Gambling* recounts how Matthews got tangled in an FBI sting in the early 1980s. He was accused of taking $14,000 in bribes from an undercover FBI agent, and he allegedly conspired to extort $668,000 from businesses the FBI had set up. Matthews pleaded guilty in 1984 to extortion, admitting he took $10,000 from an FBI agent, and went to prison.

Prior to pleading guilty, Matthews had been recalled from office and replaced by Usry, who had been a school administrator. Matthews, who is white, had won the mayoral election over Usry, who is black, by 354 votes. Racial tensions already ran high in the city, but after that mayoral race, they were supercharged and culminated in the recall effort that began the day Matthews was inaugurated as mayor.

Usry, too, had legal problems. He was caught up in a New Jersey State Police undercover investigation of payoffs for city building approvals. The now-discredited investigation came to be called COMSERV because the alleged bribes were referred to as a performance of "community service," as in a person would pay so much in community service to secure approval for a particular project. Usry pleaded guilty to a minor charge, entered a pretrial-intervention program and ultimately had his record expunged.

As mayor, Usry wanted to bring people back to Atlantic City, not only as tourists, but also as residents. Like the beach grasses that hold dunes together, Usry believed the residents would offer the city a sense of stability and community, and he undertook the reclamation of the Northeast Inlet section of town. Whelan, his successor, has continued Usry's work and welcomed family-oriented activities to the city as well.

State law requires casinos to hand over some of their profits to help pay for projects throughout the state, including reinvestment in Atlantic City. This has allowed the Naughty Queen to trade decadence for diversity, and round out her gaming-hall offerings with wholesome attractions like the Ocean Life Center aquarium and the Sandcastle baseball stadium, home to the minor-league Atlantic City Surf team, as well as the restored Absecon Lighthouse. In addition, the city makes a stunning first impression at the base of the Atlantic City Expressway with a new convention center.

The infusion of casino money has permitted Atlantic City to rebuild, literally. Land in the Northeast Inlet, prime real estate that had fallen to overt drug dealing and dilapidated crack houses, was cleared out and cleaned up so that condominiums, town houses and single-family homes could be built.

And the people are coming back. Atlantic City's population of 66,000 in the 1930s had dropped to a low of 37,986 by the 1990 census. Ten years later, the U.S. Census Bureau counted 40,517 people living in the city.

The Queen's new and younger subjects find today's casino hotels glamorous and spectacular. Old-timers recall more intimate gaming places, an air of congeniality, the personal touch and the seemingly unlimited generosity of the bosses. They claim legal restrictions create a frigid, stilted environment.

But thirty-three million tourists a year disagree. And so does the Queen. Her naughtiness may have been tamed, but she also saw the old ways were relics and that she, too, would become one if she did not change. She, as much as anyone else, chose to vest herself in legitimacy — and then find a new way to have a good time.

Acknowledgements

M y heartfelt thanks go to Vicki Gold Levi, Atlantic City's unofficial historian, for her support and friendship during my "endurance run" of rejections. Her faith in my ability lifted my spirits. Her love for Atlantic City has never wavered, even during bad times.

I offer special thanks to John Stoneburg, who wrote an unpublished biography of Enoch "Nucky" Johnson with Nucky's approval. I also wish to thank Harry Duke, who wrote and self-published *Neutral Territory,* a book about Atlantic City's rackets during the twenties and thirties.

I give special thanks to Carole Langer, a highly skilled producer with the *Arts & Entertainment Network,* and to her partner, Luke Sacher, whose talents as a photographer are appreciated.

Thanks also to Susan Pollock, an Atlantic City native and television producer, whose efforts on my behalf through the years truly have been appreciated.

I thank the following people, who graciously supplied me with photographs, information and interesting stories:

Harold Abrams for his collection of stories and the use of his photographs; Marie Boyd for her enthusiasm for my project and for the use of photographs she and her husband, Jimmy, have collected; Robert Ruffolo Jr. for his assistance and patience and the use of his photographs; Ed Hallowell for permission to use his photographs; Syd Stoen, a well-known photographer, for the use of his photographs; Ray Herbert, also known as "Panorama Ray," for his kindness; Mike Blizzard, a well-known Atlantic County photographer; Bill Mark, who photographed Frank Sinatra and Skinny D'Amato and his friends; Fred Hess & Son, Atlantic City photographers, whom I believe photographed just about every inch of the Absecon Island; and Al Gold, Vicki's father, whose lips pressed Marilyn Monroe's cheek.

Other photographers I wish to thank include: Central Studios; Virginia Woodhouse; Max Learn; Ace Alegna; and Gregg Kohl.

I also would like to acknowledge the following: *The Press of Atlantic City*; Potsie from New York City; George Evans Associates; Maurice Seymour; and Atlantic Photo Center, with special thanks to Marlene Armstrong and Mike Sciullo, who is, in particular, an extraordinary man.

Through my years of work on this book, I have spoken to many islanders who have related stories about the Naughty Queen and her subjects, including the following: Jules Blumberg; Carol Blumberg; Alia Sayegh; Millie and Charles Siciliano; Kay Di Giacinto; Betty Nigro Orr; Richard "Smitty" Smith; Betty and Frank Gitto; Edna Dehn Lucia; Louis Schwartz; Connie and Augustine Lazaro; Mitzi and Harry Stein; Raymond "Seven-Seven" Harris; artist Louis Levine, also known as "Boardwalk Louie"; Ellen Baldwin; Barbara Barab Levitt; Rose and Doug Scogno; Betty Ann Puggi; Jane Sullivan; Dana Bader Casey and Bill Casey; and Ralph Meshon.

Thanks to the Atlantic City Free Public Library and its reference staff, especially to Julie Senack, who were helpful in so many ways. Thank you to the Margate Public Library and its staff for their assistance. And thanks to Dr. William J. Morrow for his kindness.

Special recognition is due to Jack Bradley, a friend of Skinny and Willie's, who became my friend as well. Jack died of a heart attack at eighty-four years of age on August 30, 2001. I wish he would have lived to see the publication of my book. Jack was exuberant about my project, and he had an acuity about dates and names that amazed me. Thanks, Jack.

To Ray Fisk, my publisher and a class act, a special thanks. He believed in my project when he read the book in July 2000.

I'd like to thank the publisher's research assistant, Rachel Bara, whose talents and instincts were invaluable to me, and this book's designer, Leslee Ganss, for her incredible work; her talent is truly appreciated.

And overwhelming gratitude to my editor, Peggy Ackermann, who has brought out the best in me with her excellent editing, which was never didactic but always encouraging.

Selected Bibliography

For the benefit of readers who would like to know more about celebrities and Atlantic City history and gambling, before and after legalization, the following selection of books is provided. Most of these books were used while researching *Chance of a Lifetime*. Also included are the names of the periodicals that were used as sources.

Buchholz, Margaret Thomas, ed. *Shore Chronicles: Diaries and Travelers' Tales from the Jersey Shore, 1764-1955*. Harvey Cedars, N.J.: Down The Shore Publishing, 1999.

Cramer, Richard Ben. *Joe DiMaggio: The Hero's Life*. New York: Simon & Schuster, 2000.

Davis, Ed. *Atlantic City Diary: A Century of Memories, 1880-1985*. McKee City, N.J.: (self-published) Atlantic Sunrise Publishing Co., 1980.

Duke, Harry. *Neutral Territory*. Philadelphia, Pa.: (self-published) Dorrance & Co., 1977.

Frank, William E. and Joseph W. Burns. *The Case of Enoch L. Johnson: A Complete Report of the Atlantic City Investigation*. New Jersey: United States Treasury Department and the Department of Justice, 1943.

Funnell, Charles E. *By the Beautiful Sea: The Rise and High Times of That Great American Resort*. New Brunswick, N.J.: Rutgers University Press, 1983.

Gabler, Neal. *Winchell: Gossip, Power and the Culture of Celebrity*. New York: Alfred A. Knopf Inc., 1994.

Johnston, David. *Temples of Chance*. New York: Doubleday, 1992.

Kuntz, Tom, ed. and Phil Kuntz, ed. *The Sinatra Files*. New York: Three Rivers Press, 2000.

Levi, Vicki Gold and Lee Eisenberg. *Atlantic City: 125 Years of Ocean Madness.* New York: Clarkson N. Potter Inc., 1979.

Levy, Shawn. *King of Comedy.* New York: St. Martin's Press, 1996.

Lloyd, John Bailey. *Six Miles At Sea: A Pictorial History of Long Beach Island.* Harvey Cedars, N.J.: Down The Shore Publishing, 1990.

McMahon, William. *So Young ... So Gay!* Atlantic City: Atlantic City Press, 1970.

National Reporter System. *The Atlantic Reporter.* St. Paul, Minn.: West Publishing Co., 1931.

Pollock, Michael. *Hostage To Fortune: Atlantic City and Casino Gambling.* Princeton, N.J.: Center for Analysis of Public Issues, 1987.

Riverol, A.R. *Live from Atlantic City: The History of the Miss America Pageant Before, After and in Spite of Television.* Bowling Green, Ohio: Bowling Green State University Popular Press, 1992.

Roberts, Russell and Rich Youmans. *Down the Jersey Shore.* New Brunswick, N.J.: Rutgers University Press, 1993.

Sinatra, Tina. *My Father's Daughter.* New York: Simon & Schuster, 2000.

Souder, H. J., ed. *Who's Who in New Jersey, Atlantic County Edition.* New York: National Biographic News Service, 1925.

Taraborrelli, Randy J. *Sinatra: Behind the Legend.* Secaucus, N.J.: Carol Publishing Group, 1997.

Newspapers and Magazines

The Press of Atlantic City, which has gone by several names since its founding, including: *Atlantic City Daily Press, Atlantic City Press, The Press* and currently, *The Press of Atlantic City.*
Camden Courier-Post
New York Post
New York Journal
The New York Times
The Philadelphia Daily News
The Philadelphia Inquirer
Philadelphia Magazine
The Saturday Evening Post
The Absecon Sun

Advertisement for Dean Martin and Jerry Lewis, when they were appearing separately, 1946.

Index

Down The Shore Publishing *specializes in books, calendars, cards and videos about New Jersey and the Shore. For a free catalog of all our titles or to be included on our mailing list, just send us a request:*

Down The Shore Publishing
Box 3100, Harvey Cedars, NJ 08008

or visit our website at
www.down-the-shore.com